Outlines on Bible Characters

Outlines on Bible Characters

Croft M. Pentz

BAKER BOOK HOUSE
Grand Rapids, Michigan 49516

ISBN: 0-8010-7108-9

Second printing, December 1992

Printed in the United States of America

Contents

New Testament Characters

Old Testament Characters

1

Adam and Eve—God's Creation

Genesis 2:1–25

Man was created by God; he was created in the image of God. God created man for fellowship. Man did not evolve from a monkey! When he created man, God gave him a soul. Since man has a soul, he may communicate with God.

I. The Creator—God (vv. 1–3)

A. The results (v. 1). The heavens and the earth were created by God. All things created by him (John 1:3).

B. The rest (v. 2). God blessed the seventh day, making it a day of rest. The body needs one day of rest per week.

C. The remembrance (v. 3). After the Lord's resurrection the disciples kept Sunday as a day of rest. It is called the Lord's Day. Jesus repeated all the Ten Commandments in the New Testament, except the one that commands keeping the sabbath. See Acts 20:7, 1 Corinthians 16:2, and Revelation 1:10.

II. The Creation—Man (vv. 4–14)

A. Conditions (vv. 4–6). No rain. The ground was watered by a certain kind of mist. Later when Noah said it would rain, the people didn't believe him (Gen. 6–8).

B. Creation (v. 7). God created man from the dust of the ground. When God breathed into man, man became a soul.

III. The Condition—Work (vv. 15–17)

A. Work (v. 15). Man was given the responsibility of caring for the garden. God puts strong emphasis on work (Rom. 12:11). See Ecclesiastes 9:10.

B. Warning (v. 16). Man was given freedom of choice. If he disobeyed, he would die. Compare with Mark 16:16.

C. Wrong (v. 17). If man partook of the tree, he would be separated from God. Note the words of Joshua 24:15.

IV. The Companion—Woman (vv. 18–25)

A. Purpose (vv. 18–20). It was not good for man to live alone. God would provide a helpmate. Note Genesis 12:24.

B. Plan (vv. 21–23). Eve was taken from Adam's rib. Not from his foot to be trampled upon . . . not from the head to top her . . . but from his side to be near his heart, and to stand side by side. They would stand as *one*!

C. Personality (v. 24). Two people come together in marriage and become *one*. No longer me and mine, but *ours*. In the word *wedding* the *we* comes before the *I*.

D. Perfection (v. 25). Though Adam and Eve were naked, they were not ashamed. They were innocent.

We are not fulfilling God's will until we fellowship with God. We cannot fellowship with God until we are born again (John 3:1–8). When we are born again, we are in God's family (John 1:12; 1 John 3:2). We need to live daily in fellowship with God (1 John 1:7).

2

Eve—the First Mother

Genesis 1:27–28; 2:18–24; 3:20

Eve was the first woman, first wife, first mother. She was the mother of all living. She was the first sinner (Gen. 3:1–6). She sinned, then Adam followed. Their first two children (Cain and Abel) were different in character. Abel served God—Cain rejected God! Eve saw her sin and repented. Too many people look at the failure and the negative part of the sinner—not the repentance and the positive.

I. The Divine Purpose (1:27, 28)

A. Creation—"And God said, 'Let us make man in our image, after our likeness.'" Man was made in God's image. God is a Spirit (John 4:24). God created man and gave him a living soul (Gen. 2:7). Jesus spoke of losing our soul (Mark 8:36).

B. Control—"And let them have dominion over the fish of the sea, and over the fowl of the air, and over the cattle, and over every creeping thing that creepeth upon the earth." What a privilege—what a responsibility!

C. Command (v. 28). Both Adam and Eve as one were given responsibilities. They would work together. To work together, both must agree (Amos 3:3).

II. The Divine Plan (2:18–24)

A. Plan (v. 18). It is not good for man to be alone. He needs a helper. Later Adam will be given a wife. God created man for fellowship.

B. Problem (vv. 19–20). Though Adam was busy, he was not satisfied.

C. Provision (vv. 21–24).
   1. Creation. Eve was taken from Adam's rib, near his heart . . . side by side . . . not from his head to top him . . . not from his foot to be trampled by him . . . but near his heart to be loved.
   2. Cooperation. Note v. 24, "Shall be one flesh." One in prayer, plans, and work. Now it is "Ours"! In the word *wedding*, the *we* comes before the *I*!

III. The Divine Provision (3:20)

A. Provision of a woman. Man needed a "helpmeet." Every home needs a woman. Adam needed a woman. He needed a wife.

B. Plan of the woman (Gen. 2:18). Note the description of an ideal wife in Proverbs 31:10–31. The strength of any home, community, or nation depends on the home.

C. Pardon through woman (Gen. 3:15). Through the "seed of the woman" Satan would be defeated and destroyed. Compare with Isaiah 7:14 and Matthew 1:18–23.

Eve repented of her sin. Note Genesis 4:1, "I have gotten a man from the LORD." Though her son Cain killed Abel, she had another son named Seth, meaning, "called." The name also means, "appointed, given for a set purpose." God forgives all sin when we repent. Note the words of Psalm 103:3. All human beings fail and have shortcomings. Note the word of hope in 1 John 2:1, 12.

3

Cain—the First Murderer

Genesis 4:1–17

Cain and Abel were the first children born in this world. They had good and godly parents. The children knew right from wrong. God gave them freedom of choice. Abel chose what is right and Cain chose what is wrong. Though there was no written Bible, not even the Ten Commandments, Cain knew what was right and wrong.

I. The Children (vv. 1–5)

A. First children (vv. 1–2). Cain was a farmer. Abel was a shepherd.

B. First consecration (vv. 3–4). Cain brought the fruit of the ground. Abel brought a lamb. Cain's way was man's way; Abel's way was God's way. Man must come God's way, since there is no other way (John 14:6; Acts 4:12).

C. First contempt (v. 5). God accepts Abel's gift, but rejects Cain's. Cain becomes angry. Had Cain obeyed God, his gift would have been accepted. God wants us to obey him (John 14:15). We may not understand, but we must obey.

II. The Circumstances (vv. 6–8)

A. Attitude (v. 6). God asks Cain why he is sad. Disobedience always brings sadness and loneliness. It affects our attitudes and affections. See Proverbs 23:7.

B. Acceptance (v. 7). If we obey God and do things his way, we will be accepted. If we reject, it will lead to other sins. Note how stubbornness is equal to idolatry (1 Sam. 15:23).

C. Anger (v. 8). Cain's jealousy leads to hatred and anger. Later these feelings lead to murder. Anger confuses the mind. People cannot think properly when they are angry.

Homes are broken because of jealousy and anger. See the answer to this sad condition in James 1:19.

III. The Consequences (vv. 9–17)

A. Sin (v. 9). Cain thought he could hide his sin. He pretended he didn't know where Abel was, though he had just killed him. The Bible says our sins will find us out (Num. 32:23). We cannot hide from God! See Revelation 20:11–15.

B. Shame (v. 10). Abel's blood cries out from the ground. The death of Abel would constantly convict Cain.

C. Sorrow (vv. 11–12). Note the suffering of Cain:

   1. The ground was cursed. It would not produce good crops for Cain.
   2. Cain would be a fugitive. He would wander from place to place and have no permanent home. He would have no peace. The wicked have no peace (Prov. 11:21, 31).

D. Suffering (vv. 13–15). Cain's suffering seemed more than he could bear. Many people would seek to kill Cain. God places a mark on Cain's forehead so people would not kill him.

E. Separation (vv. 16–17). Cain leaves the presence of God. There is no word that he repented. The wages of sin is death or separation from God. See Romans 3:23 and Ezekiel 18:4.

Wrong choices always lead to sin. Note Cain chose to disobey, to be jealous, to hate, to become angry, and to kill. God gives us the power of choice. Cain became what he was by choice. Because of wrong choices, he paid for his sin. We cannot sin habitually without paying for it.

4

Noah—the Ark Builder

Genesis 6:5–22; 7:1–24

Man was created as perfect by God. Sin destroyed this perfection (Gen. 3). This sin grew until God was sorry he created man. The whole earth was filled with sin. Sin displeases God. It separates man from God. God's judgment must fall on sin (Rev. 20:11–15). Sin separates from God (Ps. 66:16). Before God sends judgment on sin, he always warns the sinner. The people had 120 years to repent and change their ways in Noah's time (Gen. 3:15).

I. The Problem (6:5)

A. Greatness of sin—"Wickedness of man was great in the earth."

B. Grief of sin—"That every imagination of the thoughts of his heart was only evil continually." See Jeremiah 17:9.

II. The Plan (6:6–7)

A. Problem (v. 6). God was sorry he created man. When he created man, he was pleased. See Genesis 1:31. Now he is sorry he created man.

B. Plan (v. 7). God says he will destroy all the people and creation. God must deal with sin and destroy it. He gave man opportunity to repent (Gen. 6:3).

III. The Person (6:8–9)

A. Person (v. 8). Nothing is said of Noah until he was 500 years old. He lived to be 950 (Gen. 9:29). Noah's grandfather was Methuselah, the oldest man who ever lived (Gen. 5:27).

B. Personality (v. 9). Note two things about Noah. He was a just man—meaning he lived right. He was a perfect man—

this does not mean sinless perfection. See also Matthew 5:48.

IV. The Plight (6:10–13)

A. Degradation of the earth (vv. 10–12). Note that the earth was corrupt. It was sinful. God created man perfect. After Adam and Eve's sin, all were born in sin (Rom. 5:12, 19).

B. Destruction of the earth (v. 13). An estimated 137 million people lived on the earth at this time. God who created man now would destroy man. Sin always brings separation. See Romans 6:23. According to the Scofield Bible 1,651 years passed from creation until this time.

V. The Preparation (6:14–22)

A. Size of the ark (vv. 14–16). *The Living Bible* says the ark was 450 feet long, 75 feet high, 45 feet wide. It was three stories high. It had just one window.

B. Safety in the ark (vv. 17–22). Only those in the ark were safe. Only those born again will be in heaven (John 3:1–8).

VI. The Protection (7:1–24)

A. Design (vv. 1–16). The animals went two by two into the ark, except the sheep—there were seven of these for sacrifices.

B. Death (vv. 17–24). It rained forty days and nights. All living creatures outside the ark died. Rejection means death (Mark 16:16).

Are you in Christ? If not, you are not safe. Accept him as your Savior and you are safe (John 5:24). The last days before Christ returns to earth will be similar to those of Noah. See Matthew 24:37–44. Note v. 44. Be sure to be in Christ!

5

Remember Lot's Wife

Genesis 13:12–13, 19:1–26

Jesus referred to this passage when he said, "Remember Lot's wife" (Luke 17:32). Sodom and Gomorrah were two sinful cities. There were not ten righteous people in these cities. There are many lessons to learn from Lot's wife. Here are just a few: (1) She loved the world more than God; (2) she tried to serve two masters (See Matthew 6:24); (3) she thought she could live as she pleased.

I. Remember Her Desire (13:12)

A. Sinful desire. She loved sin more than God. Look how people love darkness rather than light (John 3:19).

B. Selfish desire. She did not learn self-discipline. God's Word teaches self-discipline (1 Cor. 9:27).

C. Sensual desire. Note the works of the flesh (Gal. 5:19).

II. Remember Her Danger (13:13)

A. Holy control. Lot and his family moved close to Sodom and soon were living there. Compare with 2 Corinthians 6:17.

B. Bad company. Christians need Christian friends. See Amos 3:3; 2 Corinthians 7:1.

III. Remember Her Degradation (19:1–14)

A. Unnatural desires (vv. 1–13). Note how God gave up these people (Rom. 1:27, 28). This sin is immoral, it is not normal.

B. Un-Christian influence (v. 14). Lot's sons-in-law didn't accept his words. He was a poor example.

IV. Remember Her Destruction (19:15–25)

A. An angel comes to deliver Lot's family from destruction (v. 15). Christ delivers us (John 8:32, 36).
B. Lot and his family didn't want to leave (v. 16). They loved sin more than God (2 Tim. 3:4).
C. They were told not to look back (v. 17). See Luke 9:62.
D. God destroys the cities with fire and brimstone (vv. 18–25). Only Lot and his daughters escape.

V. Remember Her Doom (19:26)

A. Judgment on stubbornness. Lot's wife looks back and becomes a pillar of salt. What God says, he means!
B. Judgment on sin (Rom. 6:23). Man is a sinner by birth. He remains a sinner by choice.
C. Judgment on self-righteousness (John 3:1–8).

God gives us this lesson to learn from it. One who truly loves God will not love the world. Lot's wife did not put God first in her life. Her selfish ambitions and desires came before God. Jesus gives us good advice in Matthew 6:33. We should put him first in our lives. Remember Lot's wife, then remember God in your daily living.

6

Sarah—the Mother of a Nation

Genesis 17:15–19; 18:9–15; Hebrews 11:11, 12

God often completes his work through godly women who cooperate with their husbands. Peter tells how Sarah is a good example for women to follow (1 Peter 3:1–6). The writer of Hebrews speaks highly of her (Heb. 11:11, 12). The New Testament Jews often referred to Sarah as a good role model.

I. The Promise Given to Sarah (Gen. 17:15–19)

A. Person (v. 15). Sari's name was changed to Sarah, meaning Prince. She showed great respect toward Abraham. Sarah had a great part in the life of Abraham.

B. Promise (v. 16). God would give Abraham and Sarah a son. Sarah would be a mother of nations. If God promises something, he will keep that promise!

II. The Providing Miracle to Sarah (Gen. 18:9–15)

A. Person (vv. 9–10). Heavenly visitors come to see Abraham and Sarah. They promise Abraham and Sarah that they would indeed have a son. God cannot lie (Titus 1:2).

B. Problem (vv. 11–15)

1. Age (v. 11). It was impossible for them (Abraham, age 100, and Sarah, age 90) to have a baby. But God does more than we ask (Eph. 3:20).
2. Attitude (v. 12). "So Sarah laughed silently, 'A woman my age have a baby?' she scoffed to herself. 'And with a husband as old as mine'" (LB).
3. Answer (vv. 13–14). "Then God said to Abraham, 'Why did Sarah laugh? Why did she say, "Can an old woman like me have a baby?" Is anything too hard for God?

Next year, just as I told you, I will certainly see to it that Sarah has a son'" (LB).

4. Action (v. 15). "But Sarah denied it, 'I didn't laugh,' she lied, for she was afraid" (LB).

III. The Promise Fulfilled to Sarah (Heb. 11:11, 12)

A. Faith in God (v. 11a). As God promised, Sarah conceived and has a child. Note: "Through faith." Compare with Hebrews 11:1, 6. Waiting to see is not faith!

B. Faithful to God (v. 11b). Sarah knew God was faithful. Note promise of Numbers 23:19.

C. Faithfulness of God (v. 12). "And so a whole nation came from Abraham, who was too old to have even one child—a nation with so many millions of people that, like the stars of the sky and the sand on the ocean shores, there is no way to count them" (LB).

God did the impossible through Abraham and Sarah. God often works through impossible situations. He enjoys doing the impossible. There is no limit to what he can and will do, if he can only find the people to work through. The "God of miracles" is alive today! Allow him to do the impossible through you.

7

Abraham—a Friend of God

Genesis 18:1–5, 16–33

God visits Abraham and speaks to him. When the heavenly visitors came to Abraham, he didn't recognize them. The prophet says God made visits to the earth before he came in human flesh (Mic. 5:2). In Hebrews 11, "The Hall of Fame Chapter," six verses are given to Abraham. Abraham was called a friend of God (James 2:23). At first, his name was Abram—later it was changed to Abraham.

I. Abraham's Personal Relationship (vv 1–5)

A. Appearance (v. 1). The Lord sought for a person to do his work. He found this person in Abraham (Gen. 11:31). See also Acts 7:7, 8.

B. Angels (v. 2). Those "men" visiting Abraham were angels, but he was not aware of their heavenly origin. One was called Lord (18:1, 13, 33; 19:1). Note the power the angels had over the Sodomites (v. 13).

C. Attitude (vv. 3–5). Abraham took good care of these visitors. He practiced hospitality. Note how Christians should be given to hospitality (Rom. 12:13). Peter tells us to use hospitality one to another (1 Peter 4:9). The writer of the Book of Hebrews says by being hospitable, we may entertain angels (Heb. 13:2).

II. Abraham's Personal Revelation (vv. 16–19)

A. After completing their mission, the visitors leave (v. 16).

B. There was debate among the heavenly messengers if they should tell Abraham (v. 17). Later we shall see God speaking to Abraham (18:33).

C. Promise (vv. 18–19). "For Abraham shall become a mighty

nation, and he will be a source of blessing for all nations of the earth. And I picked him out to have godly descendants and a godly household—men who are just and good—so that I can do for him all I have promised" (LB). Abraham is to be the father of the Jewish nation.

III. Abraham's Personal Request (vv. 20–32)

A. Perversion of Sodom (vv. 20–21). "So the Lord told Abraham, 'I heard that the people of Sodom and Gomorrah are utterly evil, and that everything they do is wicked. I am going down to see whether these reports are true or not'" (LB).

B. Plan for Sodom (vv. 22–24). If there were fifty righteous souls, God would spare it. The same sin is identified in Romans 1:27. Note how God gave up on these people (Rom. 1:28).

C. Plea for Sodom (vv. 25–32). Abraham intercedes for Sodom, because Lot and his family lived there (v. 33). The Lord leaves after speaking to Abraham. Abraham goes to his own tent.

God constantly seeks people to do his work. Note the search for such individuals in Ezekiel 22:30. After salvation, all people are called to do God's work (John 15:16). As God worked through Abraham, so he will work through those who yield to him. If we follow him, he will make us what he wants us to be (Matt. 4:19). What an honor—a friend of God! A person God could trust! Let's seek to be the same.

8

Esau—the Man Without Discipline

Genesis 25:19–34; Hebrews 12:14–17

We hear the phrase, "The God of Abraham, Isaac, and Jacob." We never hear the name of Esau in this phrase. Esau was Jacob's twin brother. God could not use Esau. God uses only the people he can trust. Esau was interested in temporal blessings. He was more concerned with the moment than the eternal. Jesus spoke of sending up eternal treasures to heaven (Matt. 6:19, 20).

I. The Subjects (Gen. 19–28)

A. Children (vv. 19–23). Isaac and Rebekah were married for twenty-one years before they had children. Note: "Two nations in thy womb"—the Edomites and Israelites. The Messiah would come through Abraham, Isaac, and Jacob.

B. Character (vv. 24–27). Esau was a man of the field, a farmer. Jacob lived in tents and helped his mother with the household chores.

C. Confusion (v. 28). Isaac loved Esau and Rebekah loved Jacob. We will see later how playing favorites with the children led to problems and troubles.

II. The Selling (vv. 29–34)

A. Impatience (vv. 29–30). Esau had no self-control. His selfish desires came first. God was not first in his life. Compare with Matthew 6:33, Proverbs 3:5, 6. Note the importance of self-control in 1 Corinthians 9:27.

B. Indifference (vv. 31–34).

1. Test (vv. 31–32). Jacob knew better, but took advantage of Esau's weakness to deceive him.

2. Trade (v. 33). Esau sold his birthright for a bowl of soup. The birthright was the privilege of the firstborn. This meant a double portion of the inheritance and the leader of the home. Esau gave all this up for a bowl of soup—a momentary pleasure.

III. The Sorrow (Heb. 12:16, 17)

A. Warning (v. 16) The writer of Hebrews warns of repeating Esau's mistake, exhorting the Christian to learn from Esau's failure. Esau gave up all for his appetite. Esau was called profane, without respect for the sacred. Selfishness always causes this. See Luke 9:23.
   1. Physical appetites. Overeating. See Luke 21:34.
   2. Sexual sins. Adultery and fornication. See 1 Corinthians 6:9.
   3. Material appetite. Desire for material gain. Compare with 1 Timothy 6:10.

B. Result (v. 17). Esau lost all because he was careless. He was sorry, but it was too late. Note the wrong gain (Mark 8:36).

Esau later married heathen women. What a difference in these two—Esau and Jacob. Both had the same parents and home life. What made the difference? Choice! Children can be taught. They can be given good examples. They can be counseled and even scolded. But they will make the decision that determines their destiny. Learn to live for eternity—not for the moment.

9

Isaac—the Peacemaker

Genesis 26:12–25

Isaac was the long-desired son of Abraham. God had promised a son to Abraham (Gen. 17:15–19). God sent this promised son. Later, God would test the faith of Abraham (Gen. 22:1–14). At the time of this passage both Abraham and Sarah are dead. The Scofield Bible says Isaac is about ninety-four years old.

I. Isaac's Power (vv. 12–14)

A. Enlargement (vv. 12–13). His crops produced one hundred times more than he sowed. There was a famine in other lands. God's blessings always make us rich (Prov. 10:22). God helps and blesses us in a three-fold way: spiritually, physically, and materially.

B. Envy (v. 14). See how the Philistines envy Isaac. However, when a man's ways please God, even his enemies will be at peace with him (Prov. 16:7). The enemies envy our peace, success, and hope.

II. Isaac's Problems (vv. 15–21)

A. Persecution. Note 14b, how the Philistines envy Isaac. All the followers of Christ suffer persecution (2 Tim. 3:12). The non-Christians hate the Christ in the Christians.

B. Problems (vv. 15–17). The wells which Isaac dug were filled by his enemies. He could have stayed, fighting for his rights, but he moved on. He went the second mile. See Matthew 5:41.

C. Patience (vv. 18–21). Isaac made more wells. The Philistines fill these. The Christian must be willing to "turn the cheek" (Matt. 5:35, 42). All Christians need more patience.

1. Patience at home. Avoid arguments and misunderstandings.
2. Patience at work. Be patient with supervisors and fellow-workers.
3. Patience with enemies. Be kind—love them.
4. Patience in church. Be patient with church leaders.

D. Pity. The motto for all Christians should be Ephesians 4:32. Practice these words daily. See also Galatians 6:1–8.

III. Isaac's Promotion (vv. 22–25)

A. Peace (v. 22). Isaac moved on to other wells when the enemy took his wells. God blessed him and gave him peace. He had a choice to stay and claim his possession or leave. He left, knowing God would use this for his glory (Rom. 8:28).

B. Promise (vv. 23–24). When we follow God, we get what we need. See Philippians 4:19 and Psalm 37:25.

C. Prayer (v. 25). Isaac pauses to pray and thank God. As God blesses, thank him. See Psalm 103:1–3, and 1 Thessalonians 5:18.

All Christians should seek to be peacemakers. God says the peacemakers will be blessed (Matt. 5:9). Follow these steps.

1. Never take sides. Listen to both sides.
2. Listen carefully. Don't be in a hurry to give advice.
3. Pray for wisdom and understanding. See James 1:5.
4. Never argue or get excited. Remain calm always.
5. Don't reveal your feeling.

10

Jacob—the Deceiver

Genesis 27:1–46

Deception is wrong! It is sin! It is lying. Some other synonyms for lying are: fraud, dishonesty, perversion, distortion, counterfeiting, false pretense. Deception separates us from God. It creates many problems for those who are deceived, and for those doing the deceiving. Later we shall see Jacob suffering for his sin of deception.

I. The Desire May Lead to Deception

A. Isaac was old and wanted venison before he died. He sent Esau to get it. Esau was the older of the twin brothers (Esau and Jacob).

B. Rebekah had a deceitful plan (v. 8). Deceit destroys. It is of the devil. Note the importance of being honest (Exod. 20:16). Rebekah tells Jacob (vv. 9–10) not to kill the deer, but a goat, and deceive the father. One of Satan's favorite tools is deceit. It is lying. Note Revelation 21:8.

II. Deception May Lead to Degradation (vv. 11–29)

A. Problem (vv. 11–13). Esau was a "hairy man." Jacob was a man with "smooth skin." Rebekah tells Jacob she would take care of things, such as deceiving Jacob's father.

B. Plan (vv. 14–16). Rebekah took the goat skin and covered Jacob's arms, making him hairy like Esau.

C. Presentation (v. 17–20). Jacob presents the meat. He lies, saying "I'm Esau thy firstborn." When the father asks how he found the food so quickly, he lies, saying God helped him. Deceit brings degradation!

D. Promise (vv. 21–29). Isaac was old and could not see Jacob. He felt his arms, thinking it was Esau, and blessed him.

III. Deception Often Leads to Despair (vv. 30–46)

A. Deception (vv. 30–33). Esau returns, and discovers how Jacob had deceived him and his father.

B. Despair (vv. 34–40). Isaac had already blessed Jacob. He already made certain promises and blessings he couldn't change.

C. Despised (vv. 41–46). Esau hated Jacob. He vowed to kill him after their father died. Rebekah sent Jacob to her brother's (Laban) home for safety.

We cannot do wrong without suffering and paying for it. Note how we reap what we sow (Gal. 6:7, 8). We may suffer without sinning—but you cannot sin without suffering. Lying and deception will separate us from God. See Psalm 66:18. Our sins will find us out (Num. 32:33).

11

Joseph—a Man Saves a Nation

Genesis 37–50

Joseph was a man of God! He spent about fourteen years in an Egyptian prison. He was innocent, yet he suffered. But God's merciful hand was on Joseph, and "shewed him mercy" (39:21).

I. Joseph's Early Life

A. Joseph was despised by his brothers (vv. 1–11). The father loved Joseph more than the other brothers. Note also Joseph's dreams.

B. Joseph was deported (vv. 18–28). The brothers planned to kill Joseph but instead sold him as a slave for twenty pieces of silver.

C. Jacob was deceived (vv. 29–35). Lies are told to Jacob, saying an animal killed Joseph.

II. Joseph in Prison

A. In prison he was a leader (39:1–23). Potiphar's wife lies about him. He goes back to prison.

B. Fellow prisoners, a butler and a baker, have dreams (40:1–13). God gives Joseph understanding to interpret dreams.

C. Desire (40:14–23). Joseph's interpretation comes true. The baker is hanged. The butler is free, but forgets about Joseph.

III. Joseph as Ruler

A. Joseph is freed from prison to interpret the king's dream (41:1–16).

B. Interpretation of the king's dream (41:17–37): There will be seven good and seven bad years.

C. Reward (41:38–46). Joseph is made overseer. See vv. 17–37.
D. Responsibility (41:47–57). He helps to prepare Egypt for the coming famine.

IV. Joseph Tests His Brothers
A. Joseph meets his brothers (42:1–9, 21–23) who come to buy grain because of the famine.
B. Joseph tests his brothers (43:1–17, 29–34). He wanted to know more about his family.
C. Joseph loves his brothers (44:1–34). Though they hurt him, he loves them. See Ephesians 4:32.

V. Joseph Forgives His Brothers.
A. Fear of brothers. The brothers are fearful of Joseph (45:1–3).
B. Jacob is reunited with Joseph (47:1–12). Israel is given the best land.
C. Joyful mercy enjoined (50:15–21). The fear of the brothers of Joseph hurting them was unnecessary.

Joseph's life could be summed up in four areas: (1) He had faith in God. He didn't question God. (2) He was patient during problems. He could have become bitter. (3) He was kind and forgiving to those who wronged him. He never sought to retaliate. (4) He didn't permit bitterness toward his brothers or Potiphar's wife to enter his heart. These four things made Joseph a success.

12

God Calls Moses

Exodus 3:1–15; 4:1–2, 9–12

Israel was in bondage in Egypt. God called Moses to be a deliverer. Had a church or committee called a leader, they wouldn't have called Moses. God saw what Moses could be. He saw his dedication and dependence on God. Moses was busy working when God called him. God calls busy people. He works through such people. Compare with Romans 12:11, seeing how we should not be lazy or indifferent.

I. The Call of God (3:1–6)

A. Work (v. 1). Moses works as a shepherd. For forty years God was teaching and preparing Moses for a job. Keep in mind the anger of Moses (Exod. 2:11–12).

B. Wonder (vv. 2–3). An angel appears in a burning bush. The bush was not consumed. It was difficult for Moses to understand this.

C. Woe (vv. 4–6)

1. Call (v. 4). God calls from a burning bush. Moses responds.
2. Command (vv. 5–6). The place was holy ground. God's presence and power were in that place. Compare with Isaiah 6:1–8.

II. The Compassion of God (3:7–9)

A. Divine compassion (v. 7). About eighty years had passed from the time of Moses' birth. All this time Pharaoh oppressed Israel.

B. Divine concern (vv. 8–9).

1. Promise (v. 8). God promised deliverance. God keeps his promise (Num. 23:19).

2. Pity (v. 9). God heard their cry. He knew their oppression. see Hebrews 4:15.

III. The Commission of God (3:10)

A. Divine call (v. 10a). Moses would be sent to Pharaoh. Here is an example of Christians opposing sin. Moses would oppose Pharoah's treatment of Israel. The child of God must stand against wrong (John 15:18, 19).

B. Divine commission (v. 10b). Moses would lead Israel out of Egypt. Egypt is a type of the world. As Christians, we should lead sinners to new life in Christ (John 3:1–8, 2 Cor. 5:17).

IV. The Comfort of God (3:11–15; 4:1–2, 9–12)

A. Promise (3:11–12). He will deliver. Compare with Hebrews 13:5.

B. Person (3:13–15). God's promise to Moses to show his power.

C. Power (4:1–2, 9). We may have a portion of his power. See Philippians 4:13.

D. Personal (4:10–12) God would give Moses personal instructions.

God calls man to do his work. Some people do not live close enough to hear the call. Others hear and reject. Still others don't care about God's work or his call.

13

Miriam—a Woman of Song

Exodus 15:1–8, 19–21, Micah 6:4

Miriam was the sister of Moses and Aaron. As a young person (perhaps a teenager), she was instrumental in saving the life of Moses (Exod. 2:7–9). She was responsible for getting her mother to be a nurse for Moses. From the very start, Miriam showed leadership ability. In this passage we see her leading Israel in a time of praise and thanks to God after crossing the Red Sea. God today seeks those who will praise him.

I. The Praise to God (Exod 15:1–8)

A. Delight (v. 1). Singing because the triumph of the crossing the Red Sea. Note carefully Psalm 100, a psalm of praise.

B. Deliverance (v. 2). Note the fourfold reason to sing:

1. My strength. He gives divine strength. This comes by waiting before him (Isa. 40:31).
2. My song. Psalm 104:33 encourages us to sing praise unto the Lord.
3. My God. This could be translated, "My personal God" as David said in Psalm 23:1, "My shepherd."
4. My preparation—"I will prepare him an habitation." He will not only live in my heart—he will also have all my heart!

C. Destruction (vv. 3–8). *The Living Bible* says "The Lord is a warrior" (v. 3). He destroyed those who followed Israel into the Red Sea. Compare with Psalm 2:1–4. Note v. 4, how the Lord will laugh at those who try to overcome him.

II. The Protection by God (Exod. 15:19–21)

A. Protection (v. 19). God led Israel through on dry ground.

God protected Israel but allowed Pharaoh's army to be drowned. God protects his people. See Psalm 91.

B. Praise (v. 20). Miriam led in singing and praise to God. In God's presence there is joy (Ps. 16:11). He wants our joy to be full (1 John 1:4). Note how a merry heart will sing praise (James 5:13).

C. Protection (v. 21). Sing to the Lord because of his protection and provision. Note: "For He has triumphed gloriously." God's people too may triumph. Compare with 1 John 4:4, Romans 8:31, and John 8:32.

III. The Perseverance by God (Mic. 6:4)

A. Salvation—"For I brought thee up out of the land of Egypt, and redeemed thee out of the house of servants." He has redeemed us (Ps. 40:2). He has made us new (2 Cor. 5:17; Ezek. 36:26).

B. Service—"I sent before thee Moses, Aaron, and Miriam." God calls people to his service (Mark 16:15; John 15:16). All his people are called to do a specific ministry in God's work.

All the people join Miriam in praise unto God. God had just freed them from Pharaoh and the Egyptians. He led them through the Red Sea. The psalmist admonishes us not to forget all the Lord's benefits (Ps. 103:1). Paul tells us to give thanks in all things (1 Thess. 5:18). Singing is one of the ways we may praise the Lord! Join with Miriam in singing praise to God.

14

Joshua—Moses' Successor

Joshua 1:1–9, 16

Isaiah's prophecy of Christ in Isaiah 9:6 proclaims that his name would be Immanuel, meaning, "God with us." God is with Joshua in a special way as he takes the place of leadership Moses held. The writer of Proverbs tells how God directs those who follow him (Prov. 3:5, 6). When God calls, he provides the ability to fulfill this call.

I. The Call of Joshua (vv. 1–4)

A. Occasion (v. 1). Moses dies and Joshua is the leader.

B. Order (v. 2). Go over Jordan. Go forward. Take what belongs to you. Compare with 1 Corinthians 3:22.

C. Details (vv. 3–4) They could have all the land they walked on. God wants to give us great things (Jer. 33:3).

II. The Companionship of Joshua (v. 5)

A. Power—"There shall not any man be able to stand before thee all the days of thy life." Compare with Romans 8:31.

B. Promise—"As I was with Moses, so will I be with thee." He will give strength to do all things (Phil. 4:13).

C. Protection—"I will not fail thee, nor forsake thee." Jesus said he would never forsake us (Matt. 28:20). He will not leave us (Heb. 13:5).

III. The Courage for Joshua (vv. 6–7)

A. Strength (v. 6). Don't be weak. Be mature. Don't feel sorry for yourself. Don't make excuses. Have faith in yourself!

B. Surrender (v. 7). Surrender to God's will brings courage and success. See Romans 12:1–2.

IV. The Commandment to Joshua (vv. 8–9)

A. Scripture (v. 8). Note the importance of God's Word and what we should do. (1) Retain it. (2) Meditate on it. (3) Obey it. If we follow these simple steps, we will be a success. Compare with Psalm 119:9, 11.

B. Strength (v. 9). Note the truths in this verse: (1) Be strong. (2) Be of good courage. (3) Be not afraid. (4) Neither be dismayed. (5) The Lord is with you wherever you go.

V. The Consecration of Joshua (v. 16)

A. Doing—"All that Thou commandest us we will do." Can you say this? Are you willing to accept his will for your life? Note the words of Acts 9:6.

B. Going—"And whithersoever thou sendest us we will go." The prophet Isaiah says almost the same words (Isa. 6:8).

As Joshua placed his faith in God, so we should place our faith in him. Depend on him. He is with us. There is victory for all Christians. With God's Spirit within us, we are greater than the evil in the world (1 John 4:4). We do not face the world alone—he will be with us. He will give us the strength and power to live for him and work for him.

15

Rahab—a Sinner with Faith

Joshua 2:1–6, 9–15; Hebrews 11:31

The Book of Joshua is a book of faith and courage. In this passage we see the faith of Rahab. God would keep the promise he made to Abraham—through his descendants the Messiah would come. God works through Rahab to save the spies. Why did he work through Rahab, a sinner? Perhaps he couldn't find others to work through. God at times carries out his plan through non-Christians.

I. The Spies and Rahab (Josh. 2:1–6)

A. The command (v. 1). God protects the spies through Rahab. Many of the people of Canaan were immoral, often in the name of religion.

B. The confusion (vv. 2–3). The king of Jericho knew two men had entered the city. The authorities were seeking these two spies.

C. The covering (vv. 4–6). Rahab hides the two spies under the flax roof. The flax was placed on the roof to dry.

II. The Sincerity of Rahab (Josh. 2:9–15)

A. Faith (v. 9). Though Rahab was a sinner, she had faith in God. She believed God would give this land to the Israelites. Faith believes before it sees (Heb. 11:1, 6).

B. Faithfulness (v. 10). Rahab had heard about God's faithfulness to Israel. She heard how he parted the Red Sea; defeated the heathen nations; sent the manna, water, and many other miracles.

C. Fear (v. 11). Her heart melted as she had this fear for God in her heart. She believed this to be the true God of heaven and earth.

D. Favor (vv. 12, 13). She asks for kindness since she helped the spies. She wanted protection for herself and her family.
E. Freedom (vv. 14–15). A condition is given to Rahab to put a red cord in her window. When Israel would come to destroy the city, only her house would be saved. Compare the red cord to the blood of Christ (Heb. 9:22; 1 John 1:7).

III. The Security of Rahab (Heb. 11:31)

A. The plan of faith. It believes before it sees (Heb. 11:1). It trusts God regardless of circumstances.
B. The persistence of faith. Faith never gives up. It believes before it sees. Faith is necessary (Heb. 11:6).
C. The problem of faith. Discouragement, doubt, or distrust often weaken our faith.
D. The peacefulness of faith. It asks no questions. It leaves all things in the hands of God.

Because of Rahab's faith, she and her family were saved. Note the promise of Paul in Acts 16:31—salvation for self and family. Some Christians use their faith more than others. Some read God's Word, and have stronger faith (Rom. 10:17). Read Hebrews 11, seeing how these people had great faith in God. Then seek to have the same faith.

16

Achan—Death by Sin

Joshua 7:19–26

Achan committed sin. He continued in this sin. This sin hindered Israel from winning the battle. Sin always hinders people from having God's best. Christians should hate sin. Christians should stay as far as possible away from sin. Note the effects of sin: it deceives, destroys, and deadens. Sin always separates us from God, on earth as well as in eternity.

I. The Confession by Achan (vv. 19–20)

A. Advice (v. 19). Joshua encourages Achan to confess his sin. Hiding sin only makes matters worse. If we confess our sin, God will forgive (1 John 1:9).

B. Admission (v. 20). "I have sinned." These are the hardest words to say. One must remember:

1. All humans are sinners (Rom. 3:23).
2. All sins will be forgiven if they are confessed (1 John 1:7).
3. Suffering will come if sin is not confessed (Rom. 6:23).

II. The Coveting by Achan (v. 21)

A. "I *saw* them." Many sins are committed through the eyes. Note these words from Matthew 18:9. Lust brings sin, and sin death (James 1:14–15).

B. "I *coveted* them." He broke the tenth commandment (Exod. 20:17). Coveting always leads to other sins. An unsatisfied person is an unhappy person.

C. "I *took* them." He broke the eighth commandment (Exod. 20:15). Some people think stealing is not sin unless one is caught. Place your mind on heavenly things (Col. 3:1).

III. The Concealing by Achan (vv. 22–23)

A. Searching (v. 22). They search Achan's tent and find the stolen things. The Bible warns, "Be sure your sins will find you out" (Num. 32:23). Also remember, you reap what you sow (Gal. 6:7, 8).

B. Showing (v. 23). Sin reveals itself in: (1) the mind—thoughts are evil; (2) the speech—communication is filthy; (3) the body—actions and behavior are sinful.

IV. The Consequences of Achan (vv. 24–26)

A. Report (v. 24). Achan's sin is reported to the leaders. What was hid is now made known.

B. Results (v. 25). Achan was stoned to death. The wages of sin is death (Rom. 6:23).

C. Remembrance (v. 26). This story is a reminder that sin is a terrible thing. Note the words of Solomon (Eccles. 12:1). Solomon often repeated, "all is vanity" (Eccles. 12:8).

It is easier to follow the path of sin than to follow the path of righteousness. Jesus said the road to heaven was a narrow road (Matt. 7:13–14). Only a few would follow it. Don't hide your sin—confess it. Forsake it. He forgives all sin (Ps. 103:3).

17

Deborah—Barak—Sisera

Judges 4:1–24

God will deliver those who follow him. He uses various plans and methods to accomplish his work. In the past, he used even heathen people and nations to bring about his work. Most Christians know God's plan and will for their lives. However, often they are not willing to accept it. It is easier to find God's will than do it. Those who do God's will will be rewarded (1 John 2:17).

I. The Plea for Deliverance (vv. 1–7)

A. The sin (v. 1). Sin always displeases God. What is sin? Sin is breaking the Ten Commandments (Exod. 20:1–17). It is failing to follow the Sermon on the Mount (Matt. 5–7). All sin must be punished (Rom. 6:23; Ezek. 18:4).

B. The suffering (v. 2–3). Israelites were slaves under Sisera for twenty years. When people sow sin, they must reap more sin (Gal. 6:7–8). We always reap more than we sow.

C. The salvation (vv. 4–7). Deborah the lady judge. The judges were similar to kings, except they were chosen by God. He still chooses people to do his work. See John 15:16.

D. The Savior. Christ paid the price for our deliverance. He wants us to be free. See John 8:32, 36.

II. The Plan of Deliverance (vv. 8–16)

A. The promise (v. 8). Barak was willing to go, but not alone. Always remember that God goes with us. He is on our side. Why fear when he is with us? See Hebrews 13:6.

B. The protection (v. 9). Barak persuaded Deborah to go with him. There is strength in unity and cooperation (Ps. 133:1)

C. The people (vv. 10–12). These verses list the people who were involved.
D. The problem (vv. 13–16). Sisera was an enemy of God and Israel. Note v. 16, how God confused Sisera. It is foolish to oppose God. Man is the loser. See Psalm 9:17.

III. The Plot of Deliverance (vv. 17–24)

A. Sin (vv. 17–18). Sisera ran into the tent of Jael, the wife of Herber. Later we see how this would be his downfall. Sin starts as a small seed. It grows to destroy. See Romans 6:23.
B. Seducement (v. 19). Jael seduced Sisera, saying she was his friend. Here is a picture of Satan. He leads man along, saying "Have a good time. I am your friend." All is a lie. See John 8:44. Overcome Satan (1 John 4:4).
C. Slyness (v. 20). Jael was told by Sisera to lie for him. A person who lies will commit other sins as well. Liars will go to hell (Rev. 21:8).
D. Subdued (vv. 21–24). While Sisera slept, Jael drove a nail into his head, killing him. Sin brings death. See Romans 5:12, 19.

Only as we live according to God's teachings can we be safe. If we fully follow him, he will protect us (Ps. 91). Christ has already paid for our complete deliverance and freedom. There is power available to overcome all sin. Only through Christ may we have this deliverance. Daily with his help we will overcome. See Philippians 4:13.

18

Caleb—the Enthusiastic Man

Joshua 14:6–14

Forty-five years before this scripture passage, Caleb with Joshua and the other spies entered the land of Canaan. Now Caleb is eighty-five years old, but still filled with enthusiasm. He claimed the mountain for God. When Joshua divided the land among the twelve tribes, he gave Caleb his request. If you know something to be God's will, don't give up—keep asking. He will answer.

I. The Remembrance of Caleb (vv. 6–9)

A. Promise (v. 6). Caleb is referring to the promise of Numbers 14:24, also repeated in Deuteronomy 1:36. All God's promises are true (Num. 23:19).

B. Person (v. 7). Caleb was forty years old when he went as a spy into Canaan. He had faith the Israelites could take the land (Num. 13:30).

C. Problem (v. 8). The other spies were discouraged and had no faith that Israel could conquer Canaan (Num. 13:30–33).

D. Prediction (v. 9). Canaan would be given to Israel.

II. The Resources of Caleb (vv. 10–11)

A. Help (v. 10). God gave good health and strength these forty-five years. Some of the older people during the forty years of travel died. Caleb knew the promise of Psalm 9:14–16.

B. Health (v. 11). God gives Caleb divine health. See Exodus 15:26. Obeying these rules brings health. God wants us to be healthy (3 John 2). A healthy body brings honor and glory to God.

III. The Request of Caleb (v. 12)

A. Desire (v. 12a). Caleb wanted the mountain he had seen earlier. God wants us to ask for things. Note the steps: ask, seek, knock (Matt. 7:7–9).

B. Dependence (v. 12b). He would depend on God to drive out the enemy. In our own strength we cannot overcome evil. We need God's help and strength (Phil. 4:13). Keep in mind, without God we can do nothing (John 15:5).

C. Definite. Make your requests made known unto God (Phil. 4:6). Compare with Philippians 4:19.

IV. The Reward of Caleb (vv. 13–14)

A. God granted Caleb's request (v. 13). God does give a response to our prayers. Note the promise of James 5:16.

B. Caleb got his wish. Note how Caleb "fully followed the Lord" (v. 14). Those who follow God will be rewarded in this life and in eternity (Matt. 25:21).

Caleb left a fine example for others to follow. He had great faith in God. Faith will create excitement. Our faith should inspire others to follow God. As faith brings excitement, so doubt causes others to be discouraged. If God has promised, don't doubt. He will fulfill his promise.

19

Gideon's Faith

Judges 7:1–22

God called Gideon to defeat an enemy of Israel (Judg. 6:36–40). The enemy had 135,000 soldiers—Gideon had just 300 (Judg. 8:10). God often uses and works through the least expected people or person. Little is much when God is in it. Nothing is too hard for God to accomplish. He gets the right people to work for him. Remember Zechariah 4:6.

I. The Preparation for Victory (vv. 1–9)

A. The reduction (vv. 1–6). God tells Gideon he has too many men. Note the two-step reduction process.
   1. All the men who were afraid were told to go home. Twenty-two thousand left; ten thousand stayed.
   2. The men who lapped water like a dog were told to go home. Only 300 men drank water from their hands.

B. The readiness (vv. 7–9)
   1. Only 300 men were chosen to fight 135,000 soldiers.
   2. Special. God promises victory and keeps his promises.

II. The Promise of Victory (vv. 13–15)

A. The inspiration (v. 13). God speaks at this time through dreams. God speaks today by his Spirit. See John 16:7–13. He also speaks through his Word and his servants.

B. The interpretation (v. 14). The interpretation of the dream meant victory.

C. The influence (v. 15). Gideon worshiped the Lord and had faith. One accepts Christ by faith (Eph. 2:8, 9). One lives the Christian life by faith (Gal. 2:20). To please God, one must have faith (Heb. 11:6). Faith destroys doubt—doubt destroys faith!

III. The Plan of Victory (vv. 16–22)

A. Tools (v. 16).
   1. Trumpets. A symbol of our testimony (2 Chron. 5:12).
   2. Lamps. This speaks of our testimony (Matt. 5:15–17).
   3. Empty pitchers. Picture of emptying of self (Rom. 12:1, 2).

B. Testimony (vv. 21–22). Note: "Every man in his place." Here is the secret of success. When every Christian is in his or her place, God's work goes forward. Compare with Revelation 2:10; Matthew 24:13.

God performed this miracle because Gideon was willing to trust him. An army of 300 defeats 135,000! God can work through any person who fully yields unto him. One may feel weak, but with God there is great strength and power. In the Bible as well as in history, God took the weak and helpless and did great things through them. There must be faith in God (Heb. 11:6); self (Phil. 4:13); and others. Faith asks no questions—it simply believes.

20

Jephthah Is Unappreciated

Judges 11:1–12, 27, 29–35

Jephthah's mother was a prostitute. Children may come from an unbelieving family, yet be great Christians and leaders. Choice plus determination makes the difference.

I. Leadership Opposed (vv. 1–3)

A. The past of Jephthah (v. 1). Jephthah was not responsible for how his mother lived.

B. The persecution of Jephthah (v. 2). Because of his mother's lifestyle, he was not permitted to be a leader. We should not hold anyone responsible for the mistakes and the failures of others.

C. The plight of Jephthah (v. 3). He had to leave and live in the land of Tob. This was near Damascus.

II. Leadership's Opportunity (vv. 4–11)

A. The problem (v. 4). There was a war with the Ammonites. Ammon was a descendant of Lot.

B. The plight (vv. 5–6). Now Israel needed a leader. They wanted the man they had refused—Jephthah. Strange how we change our minds when we are in trouble and need help.

C. The persecution (vv. 7–8). Jephthah reminds them of the persecution he received.

D. The promise (vv. 9–10). If Jephthah helped them defeat Ammon, then Jephthah would be their new leader.

E. The prayer (v. 11). Jephthah did not forget God. He could have become bitter, but remembered the Lord.

III. Leadership Overcoming (vv. 12, 27–36)

A. Peace (vv. 12, 27). He sought by letter to make peace.
B. Power (vv. 28–29). Note: "The Spirit of the LORD came upon Jephthah." God wants to help and assist his people. See Psalm 46:1.
C. Promise (vv. 30–31). He made a foolish vow. Sometimes under pressure, we in haste make foolish vows before God. Jephthah didn't have to keep this foolish vow. But he did.
D. Pleasure (v. 32). God gives him victory.
E. Peril (vv. 34–35). He used his daughter as a sacrifice. In biblical times a promise was something one never broke.

God can work through people regardless of their background or family. If a person surrenders to God, he will use him or her. When God calls, he will guide (Matt. 4:19). Forget the past mistakes, faults and failures. Allow God to "work you over." He knows your weaknesses and failures. He will teach, train, and use you, if you fully surrender to God.

21

Samson—the Strong/Weak Man

Judges 16:16–3

Samson was God's superman. When God's Spirit was upon him, he did wonders. When he became indifferent, he wandered from God. As the result, he lost his hair, strength, and eyes. He was made a slave. For more information, read Judges 13–16. Two important lessons can be learned from this passage: We cannot play with sin without it affecting us; and we do not know our limitations.

I. The Sin of Samson

A. Deception (vv. 16–17). Samson willingly walked into Delilah's deceitful scheme. *The Living Bible* says she was paid the equivalent of $5,000 to find the secret of Samson's strength.

B. Destruction (vv. 18–19). Samson thought he could go so far and quit. No one knows his or her limitations. Some people do not understand the deception of sin. See James 1:14, 15.

C. Departure (v. 20). God's Spirit withdrew from Samson and he didn't know it. Christians should be filled with the Spirit (Eph. 5:18), and walk in the Spirit (Gal. 5:16).

D. Degradation. Three things destroy man: Pride, sex, and money. Satan knows your weakness and seeks to destroy you. Guard against that weakness!

II. The Slavery of Samson (vv. 21–25)

A. Punishment (v. 21). Samson not only lost his hair, he also lost his strength, eyes, and his freedom. Sin makes man a slave (John 8:34).

B. Pity (vv. 22–24). The heathen rejoiced and praised their idol. When a Christian sins he or she brings shame to God and breaks the heart of God. When a Christian sins, that leaves an impact on the non–Christian and also hurts other Christians. Others will follow your example when you sin. You do have influence.

C. Persecution (v. 25). The people make sport of Samson. Sin never shows the end; it appears beautiful at the start. The end means heartache and disappointment. See Romans 6:23.

D. Pain. Sin brings: Suffering—spiritual and bodily; (2) sorrow—physical and mental; (3) separation—from God on earth and in eternity.

III. The Salvation of Samson (vv. 26–31)

A. Petition (v. 26). The picture is dark. Now Samson asks a small boy to lead him to the pillars of the temple. He desires to make up for his sin and failure to God.

B. Persecution (v. 27). The 3,000 Philistines gathered to worship Dagon were persecuting Samson. They were heathen.

C. Plea (v. 28). Samson wanted to punish these heathen for what they had done to him and Israel.

D. Prayer (vv. 29–30). Samson asks God for help. Though he sinned, he was forgiven, but reaped the result of his sin (Gal. 6:7, 8).

E. Punishment (v. 31). The 3,000 heathen were killed.

All God's people are strong when God's Spirit comes upon them. This Spirit gives power (Acts 1:8). See also 2 Timothy 1:7. He gives strength to do all things (Phil. 4:13). Don't play with temptation—resist it. Flee temptation. Samson thought he could live as he pleased. Daily we must resist and overcome sin!

22

Ruth's Choice

Ruth 1:1–20

Though Ruth lived in an ungodly age, she was a Gentile who lived a godly life. She was in the world but not part of it. She made a decision to stand for God. God was with her. The Book of Ruth was written to show the faithfulness of God to Israel. Though Israel had passed through a time of forgetting God, there was a small group of people who loved God and served him.

I. The Particulars of Ruth (vv. 1–5)

A. The country (v. 1). Moab was east of the Dead Sea.

B. The characters (vv. 2–3). Elimelech and Naomi had two sons. The name *Naomi* means "my pleasant one." Her name appears twenty-one times in this book.

C. The circumstances (vv. 4–5). Naomi's husband dies (v. 3). Her two sons marry Moabite women: Ruth and Orpah. The two sons die. Ruth and Orpah are left widows. The name *Ruth* means "beauty." Her name appears twelve times in this book and once in Matthew 1:5.

II. The Problem Facing Ruth (vv. 6–17)

A. Problem (vv. 6–7). Naomi heard the good news the famine was over in her home country. She is now a widow. She must make a new life for herself, and decides to return to Israel.

B. Permission (vv. 8–13). Naomi gives her approval and blessing to her daughters-in-law (Ruth and Orpah) to remarry.

C. Plight (vv. 14–15). Orpah returned to her country of idol worship. It is easy to follow the crowd or to remain in familiar territory. Note the warning of 2 Corinthians 6:17.

D. Personal (vv. 16–17). Here we see Ruth's dedication and determination. It meant:
   1. Hardness. Compare with 2 Timothy 2:3.
   2. Persecution. See 2 Timothy 3:12.
   3. Determination. Compare with Joshua 24:15.
   4. Consecration. See Romans 12:1, 2.

E. Plan. Ruth's choice meant these things:
   1. Naomi's path. A righteous path. See Matthew 5:20.
   2. Naomi's living place. A holy place. See Hebrews 12:14.
   3. Naomi's association. Christian friends. See Amos 3:3.
   4. Naomi's God. The true and living God.
   5. Naomi's future. Living for God. Eternal life (John 3:16).

III. The Plan for Ruth (vv. 18–20)

A. Choice (v. 18). Naomi's example had an influence on Ruth. Our lives do influence others. See Matthew 5:14–16.

B. Confusion (vv. 19–20). Naomi goes back to Bethlehem. She remembers losing her husband and children. She thought God was unjust. Compare with Romans 8:28.

Ruth's choice cost her something. Any choice toward God will cost us something! Note the words of Luke 9:23. Choosing to follow him may mean persecution, misunderstanding and suffering. Ruth willingly followed God. As the result of this dedication, she left an impact on many. As we stand for God, we show our dedication. Others will see our love for God and follow him.

23

The Reward of Ruth

Ruth 4:1–17

Two important things are shown in this passage. (1) Ruth's faithfulness. (2) The concern of Boaz. Ruth accepted hardship and was willing to care for her aged mother-in-law. Boaz was concerned with those who worked in the fields. He ate with them. He worked with them. He sat with them. People were more important to him than money or good crops. Ruth was an ideal wife for Boaz and he was an ideal husband for her.

I. The Redemption (vv. 1–6)

A. Kinsman's responsibility (vv. 1–4). A kinsman was a relative who would redeem and buy back the relative taken as a slave.

1. Savior. Christ our Savior gave his blood to buy us back from sin and its power. He is our mediator (Heb. 9:15, 22).
2. Sin. By birth, all people are slaves to sin (Rom. 3:23, Isa. 53:6). Christ is the only way of forgiveness. See John 14:6, Acts 4:12. He cleanses from all sin (1 John 1:7).

B. Kinsman's response (vv. 5–6). Boaz was the "goel kinsman," meaning he would redeem Ruth. Her relatives were too poor to redeem her. Boaz accepts this responsibility. We cannot redeem ourselves (Eph. 2:8, 9). God's hand was on Ruth and Boaz. Read carefully Proverbs 3:5–6; Psalm 37:23.

II. The Redeemer (vv. 7–12)

A. The sign (vv. 7–8). The custom of removing the shoe was making agreement, similar to shaking hands. Boaz would buy the land and redeem Ruth.

B. The sacredness (vv. 9–12). Boaz prepares to marry Ruth. Marriage is sacred and ordained of God. See Genesis 2:18, 24; Mark 10:9; Ephesians 5:21–29. All couples need to work on making stronger Christian marriages.
C. The salvation (1 Peter 1:18–19). Christ is the only Redeemer. Our good works cannot save us (Eph. 2:8, 9).

III. The Reward (vv. 13–17)

A. The son (v. 13). There is a joy in having children. With the joy comes responsibility. Proverbs 22:6; Deuteronomy 31:12–13. Children are the gift of God (Gen. 33:5; Ps. 127:3).
B. The servant (vv. 14–15). Naomi thanks and praises God for his goodness and blessings. We should always give thanks and praise (1 Thess. 5:18).
C. The salvation (vv. 16–17). Naomi's grandson, is Ruth's son, Obed, the father of Jesse who is the father of David. This son is a link in the family from which the Messiah would come (Matt. 1:5).

The price has been paid for our redemption but we must accept that redemption. Though we are born in sin (Rom. 3:23), through the blood of Christ, we have forgiveness of sin (1 John 1:7; Ps. 103:3). As we accept this pardon we become the sons and daughters of God (John 1:12). Because we are his children, some day we will be like him (1 John 3:2). Some day we will be with him (John 11:25, 26).

24

Hannah's Prayer and Dedication

1 Samuel 1:9–18, 24–28; 2:1

Samuel was the last of the judges. The judges were similar to the kings. Samuel was a man of prayer. He had a godly mother. There is no limit to the impact a godly parent makes on a child. In this passage we see the prayer and dedication of Samuel's mother, Hannah. What an example for all mothers!

I. The Perseverance of Hannah (1:9–18)

A. Sorrow (vv. 9–10). Hannah was childless. This was considered a curse in ancient Israel.

B. Situation (v. 11). Hannah prays asking God for a son. She promised to give him back to God. He would be a Nazarite. See Numbers 6:1–8, 13–21, for the characteristics of a Nazarite.

C. Sincere (vv. 12–13). Hannah was praying without words. Compare with Romans 8:26. Prayer is more than words! It is attitude. It is desire. It is a deep inner desire. It is reaching out to God even in the subconscious.

D. Sorrow (vv. 14–16). Eli is critical, saying Hannah is drunk. He could not discern spiritual behavior from non-Christian.

E. Sadness (vv. 17–18). Hannah was filled with sorrow and sadness that Eli had misjudged her.

II. The Presentation by Hannah (1:24–28)

A. Delight (1:20). God sends Hannah a son. Her prayer for a son was not selfish, but for the glory of God.

B. Dedication (vv. 24–25). Hannah and her husband bring Samuel to the temple for dedication. It is a good practice for all parents to dedicate their children to God.

C. Desire (v. 26). Hannah remembers her desire in the temple (vv. 11–13). God does answer prayer (Jer. 33:3).
D. Divine (vv. 27–28). God answers Hannah's prayer. He answers all prayers. God's delays are not denials.

III. The Praise by Hannah (2:1)

A. Practice. Prayer and praise should go together. As a bird needs both wings to fly properly, so the child of God needs both prayer and praise.
B. Prayer—"And Hannah prayed." When you need help—pray! If you are in trouble—pray! Don't wait until the trouble and problems come. Pray every day. Be prepared. See James 5:16. Remain in the attitude of prayer.
C. Praise—"My heart rejoiceth in Thee." The Bible has much to say about praise. The child of God should practice Psalm 100 daily.

We need more mothers like Hannah who give their children to God, mothers who put God first in their lives. As the result of Hannah's dedication, Samuel became one of the great giants in Israel. A nation can be no stronger than its parents. When we have godly parents we will have a godly nation. The strength of the nation and church begins in the home with the parents.

25

Eli—the Backslidden Father

1 Samuel 2:27–36

God rejects those who reject him. Eli knew better. What a poor example! Why do people reject God? There are many reasons. Here are four: indifference, selfishness, disobedience, and lack of dedication. Too many people feel they can reject God without suffering for it. The Bible says what we sow we will reap (Gal. 6:7, 8). The reaping could be years in coming—but it will come.

I. God's Reminder to Eli (vv. 27–28)

A. Divine revelation (v. 27). God speaks through the prophet. Today he speaks through the spirit, his Word and his servants. Judgment must begin with God's people (1 Peter 4:17).

B. Divine reminder (v. 28). God reminds Eli that he misused the privileges of being a priest. Eli practiced sacred things without being holy. God demands that his people be holy (Heb. 12:14).

II. God's Rejection of Eli (vv. 29–34)

A. Peril (v. 29). Sacrifices were being used in the wrong way. The cults came into being because people wanted to do things "their way"—not God's way! There's only one way (John 14:6; Acts 4:12). God's ways are different from man's (Isa. 55:8).

B. Problem (v. 30). Those who honor God will be honored by him. Reject him and he rejects you (Mark 16:16).

C. Punishment (v. 31). God will destroy the power and influence of Eli's family! What a disgrace and shame. Once servants of God, now forsaken by God. See Genesis 6:3.

D. Plight (v. 32). There would be distress and sorrow. The wages of sin is death (Rom. 6:23).
E. Perish (vv. 33–34). Later we shall see God's punishment on Eli and his sons. See again Galatians 6:7, 8.

III. God's Revelation to Eli (vv. 35–36)

A. Promise (v. 35). God would raise up a faithful priest, Samuel. Samuel would be faithful, sure, and anointed. Eli lost these important things. There is always a man "sent from God" to do his work. See John 1:6.
B. Powerful (v. 36). Everyone would bow before this new leader. He would be sent from God. Man serves God and passes, but God's work goes forward. See Matthew 16:18.
C. Permanence. Some people may weaken God's work, but they can't destroy it. His work will go forward.

God is holy and demands that his people and servants live a holy life (Lev. 10:10). God's people should cleanse themselves from all sin (2 Cor. 7:1). Only the pure in heart will see God (Matt. 5:8). Note how nothing unholy will enter heaven (Rev. 21:27). Holiness is something we should practice daily.

26

Samuel Is Obedient to God's Call

1 Samuel 3:1–10, 16–20

Samuel was living with Eli at the temple. He was a young boy, probably about twelve years old. His mother, Hannah, promised to give him to the Lord (1 Sam. 1:11, 20). He grew up in a godly home (1 Sam. 1:28; 2:26). Eli was living a backslidden life. Seeing a person such as Eli could have discouraged Samuel, but God was with him, helping him.

I. The Serious Situation (vv. 1–3)

A. Service (v. 1). There were no active prophets to warn the people. Today we have God's Word to guide us (Ps. 119:105).

B. Surrender (v. 2). Eli was getting old. His eyes were dim. Someone would have to replace him as the spiritual leader. God always seeks such a person (Ezek. 22:30).

C. Spirituality (v. 3). The candlestick on the stand in the Temple was a picture of God's presence. See Exodus 25:31–37; 27:20–21. Now God's Spirit had withdrawn from the temple. God's presence and power remains only with those who remain in him. Eli had forsaken God and God's Spirit had withdrawn. Compare with Genesis 6:3.

II. The Sacredness of Samuel (vv. 4–10)

A. Call of God (vv. 4–8). God speaks to Samuel. Samuel didn't know it was the voice of God. God does speak to man. See Isaiah 6:1–8. However, many are spiritually deaf. Others hear, but refuse to listen.

B. Counsel of Eli (v. 9). Eli says, "If you hear this voice again, say, 'Speak, Lord, for thy servant heareth.'" There are many voices calling us: A voice of fame, a voice of success, a voice of riches. These calls often drown out the voice of God.

C. Consecration of Samuel (v. 10). Samuel is open to God's call. See Isaiah 6:1–8. Note Isaiah's response to his call.

D. What constitutes a call to God's work?
   1. A burden and vision for a certain place of ministry.
   2. The ability to learn the language of the people.
   3. The open door of ministry to these people.

III. The Spirituality of Samuel (vv. 16–20)

A. Concern (vv. 16–17). God calls people at all ages; Samuel listens.

B. Complete (v. 18). Samuel tells Eli about God's message. Eli encourages Samuel to follow fully the Lord and his call. The disciples follow the same pattern (Matt. 4:19).

C. Consecration (v. 19). Samuel grew spiritually. He was willing to learn. Christians should grow and mature in the Lord (2 Peter 3:18).

D. Control (v. 20). All people from the north (Dan) to the south (Beersheba) know that God is with Samuel.

Why was Samuel a success in the eyes of God as well as man? (1) Obedience unto God. (2) A desire to learn. (3) Total dedication to God. Samuel could have taken the easy way and lived as he pleased. He was willing to follow the Lord all the way, even if it meant suffering and hardship. Obedience is the key to success.

27

Saul—the Chosen King

1 Samuel 9:3, 19–21; 10:1, 5–7, 21–22, 26–27; 11:1–2, 6–7

Samuel didn't fully agree with Israel's request for a king. Despite the fact that Israel forgot God, still he remembers them. Israel did not practice the perfect will of God. Paul spoke of God's will in three steps (Rom. 12:1, 2): good, acceptable, perfect.

I. The King Appointed (9:3, 19–21)

A. Surrender (v. 3). Saul didn't seek to be king. He was busy seeking lost animals. God works through ambitious people. Note the words of Paul in Romans 12:11.

B. Simplicity (vv. 19–21). Saul was a very simple person. He was not seeking to make a name for himself. Note the importance of humility (1 Peter 5:5, 6).

II. The King Anointed (10:1, 5–7)

A. Choice (v. 1). Samuel anoints Saul. The anointing was a sign of God's approval. The oil is a symbol of the Holy Spirit. All Christians are to be filled with the Spirit (Eph. 5:18).

B. Charge (v. 5). Saul would prophesy. God still speaks through people. Note his words to Joshua (Josh. 1:5).

C. Change (v. 6). The Spirit would come upon Saul and he would be a new man. Note the change in people when God comes into their lives (2 Cor. 5:17).

D. Call (v. 7). The Spirit of God confirmed the claim of God upon Saul's life. The Holy Spirit changes people. It changed Peter from a reed to a rock. See Acts 2:37–47.

III. The King Announced (10:21–22, 26–27)

A. Reality (vv. 21–22). Saul had faith that God had called him. He was not fearful. He knew God personally and had trusted in him.

B. Rejection (vv. 26–27). At first people didn't accept Saul as king. Note: "But he held his peace." Christ was rejected. See Isaiah 53:3; John 1:11. Be patient—you cannot satisfy all people!

IV. The King Accepted (11:1–2, 6–7, 12–14)

A. Agreement (vv. 1–2). The people seek to make an agreement with Saul. This agreement would mean compromise. One never wins by compromise. Stand for truth, even if you stand alone.

B. Anointed (vv. 6–7)
   1. Fearless (v. 6). Fearless when the Spirit came upon him. The Holy Spirit gives boldness (Acts 1:8).
   2. Fear (v. 7). The people were fearful because they could see the presence of God in the life of Saul.

C. Accepted (vv. 12–14). Finally, Saul was accepted.

We see Saul starting his reign in the proper way. However, a good start is not enough. The Bible speaks of faithfulness (Rev. 2:10). See Matthew 24:13. God's power is available for his people. He gives Christians the power to live a godly life, and also gives the power to overcome sin and the domination of Satan. Use this power to be a successful Christian.

28

Saul's Backsliding and Death

1 Samuel 15:17–26, 35; 16:14; 18:11

When Saul was chosen king, he was a man of God. God's hand was upon him. However, Saul did certain things in his life which caused him to stray from God. He became jealous of David, seeking to kill him. In the end Saul committed suicide. Some of the things that led to his backsliding are:

I. Saul's Pride (15:17)

A. Start of pride. It starts with "I"! When Christ is not first, there will be pride. See Romans 12:3.

B. Sin of pride. It separates from God.

C. Scars of pride. See Proverbs 16:18. Pride separates us from God on earth and in eternity.

II. Saul's Lying (15:18–20)

A. Purpose of lying is to hide wrong and other sins!

B. People who lie will go to hell. See Revelation 21:8.

C. Power of lying. Lying leads to other sins. It makes one a servant and slave to sin (John 8:34).

III. Saul's Disobedience (15:21–26)

A. Respect. It is better to obey than make sacrifices. It is better to obey than to be sorry. Compare with John 14:15.

B. Rebellion has two important components:

1. Rebellion is like the sin of witchcraft.
2. Stubbornness is like idolatry.

C. Rejection. Because Saul rejected God, God would reject him. See Mark 16:16. Disobedience leads to other sins.

IV. Saul's Separation (15:35)

A. He lost his fellowship with Samuel. The world and the Christian are different. Compare with Amos 3:3.

B. He lost his fellowship with God. Sin always separates from God. See Psalm 66:18.

V. Saul's Hatred (18:11)

A. Spiritual death (1 Sam. 28:15). God forsook Saul. The Spirit withdrew. Compare with Genesis 6:3. Constant rejection of Christ and the Spirit will result in the Spirit's withdrawal.

B. Physical death (1 Sam. 31:4). In the end Saul took his life. What a contrast. A man called of God, a man led of God, now destroys his life.

Unless we remain close to God, we will backslide. We cannot serve God and pleasure. Christ must be first in our lives. Jesus said one cannot serve two masters (Matt. 6:24). Unless he controls our lives, we, like Saul, will permit other things in our lives, activities which will lead us astray from God.

29

David—the Giant Killer

1 Samuel 17:4, 10–11, 20–26, 32–36, 38–54

Though David was chosen king, he had not yet taken the throne. God was preparing him for this position. God was with him and his faith grew. He killed a lion and bear with his bare hands. He did this as God's Spirit came upon him. King Saul has strayed from God. An evil spirit fills Saul. David kept a proper Christian attitude toward Saul. David would defeat Goliath, making him the champion in Israel.

I. The Defiance Toward David (vv. 4, 10–11, 20–26, 32–36)

A. Person (v. 4). Goliath was over nine feet tall.

B. Problem (v. 10). This giant challenged Israel to send a man to fight him. He was really challenging God!

C. Peril (v. 11). Israel was fearful because no one was willing to go against the giant.

D. Pity (vv. 20–26). David was filled with sorrow that no one was willing to oppose the giant and his ridicule.

E. Power (vv. 32–36). David tells how God helped him to kill the lion and bear. The same God would help him with the giant. Note carefully Philippians 4:13.

II. The Determination of David (vv. 38–47)

A. Protection (vv. 38–39). David tries Saul's armor, but it was too heavy. He couldn't depend on others and their equipment.

B. Person (v. 40). David takes his staff and five stones for his sling. He had faith in his natural abilities. He had faith in himself. He had faith in God. Note Hebrews 11:1, 6.

C. Persecution (vv. 41–43.) The giant calls David a dog. He laughs at Israel, sending a small boy to fight him.

D. Power (vv. 44–47). David warns the giant because David is coming with the power of God.
   1. Dependence (vv. 45–46). Note: "I come to thee in the name of the Lord."
   2. Deliverance (v. 46). God's deliverance. See Philippians 4:13.
   3. Dedication (v. 47). David's total dedication to God. Note: "The battle is the Lord's." He will help do his work!

III. The Defeat by David (vv. 48–54)

A. Meeting (v. 48). David didn't wait—he went to meet the giant. When we are filled with God's power, there is no fear. Compare with Acts 4:31.

B. Method (vv. 49–50). David didn't need a sword or spear to kill the giant. Just a small stone and God's help were enough to defeat the giant. God works through us (Ezek. 22:20).

C. Might (vv. 51–54). Israel was victorious. The enemy was defeated. With God's help we are powerful, we can do the impossible (Luke 1:37).

To do God's work, one must be consecrated. God takes such people and does the impossible. David later said he would fear nothing because God was with him (Ps. 23:4). Read carefully Hebrews 11, and see how God took people with dedication and performed through them. With God, the impossible becomes possible. The giants in our lives will come tumbling down.

30

David—Nabal—Abigail

1 Samuel 25:5–14, 18, 23–28, 32–33; Psalm 14:1–4

Saul's anger toward David made David run and hide. It would have been easy for David to become discouraged. Satan uses discouragement to destroy many Christians. Some Israelites didn't appreciate David's leadership, Nabal, for instance. He was rich, but had no time for God or spiritual things. David is very patient. Patience will help us overcome discouragement.

I. The Sensuality of Nabal (vv. 5–14)

A. Peace (vv. 5–6). David sends greetings to Nabal. He was not jealous of his wealth. He knew the truth of 1 Timothy 6:10.

B. Protection (vv. 7–8). David seeks help from Nabal.

C. Pride (vv. 9–12). Nabal was proud and said, "Who is David?" Simply, "David is not really important." Nabal knew Saul had sought to kill David. Nabal showed no concern or kindness toward David.

D. Problems (vv. 13–14). David loses his temper. He becomes angry. He orders his men to prepare for battle. He plans to destroy Nabal. This was not a Christian response. Personal feelings can lead many astray from God. Compare with Ephesians 4:32.

E. Person (v. 3). Nabal lived according to his name, meaning, "Foolish, careless, irreligious." His wife was fearful to speak to him. He was "churlish and evil in his doings."

II. The Stability of Abigail (vv. 18, 23–28, 32–33)

A. Person (v. 13). Abigail was the opposite of her husband, Nabal. She hurries to meet David.

B. Plea (vv. 23–28)
   1. Personal plea (vv. 23–28). She pleads with David to listen to what she has to say.
   2. Protecting plea (vv. 25–26). She tells David, "The Lord hath withholden thee from coming to shed blood." Compare with 1 Corinthians 13.
   3. Prayerful plea (v. 27). David was told to warn the younger men not to retaliate and destroy others.
   4. Pardoning plea (v. 28). Abigail seeks pardon.

C. Patience (vv. 32–33). David is thankful for Abigail's advice. This teaches him a lesson in patience.

III. The Sinfulness of Man (Ps. 14:1–4)

A. The fool (v. 1). The foolish people say, "There is no God." The word *fool* means one without sense. The foolish kill and destroy. They have no kindness or gentle feelings. See Romans 1:25–32.

B. The faith (v. 2). God looks down from heaven to see if any would trust him. He does the same today. Note many do not seek God (Rom. 1:21–23).

C. The filthy (v. 3). All people are sinners (Rom. 3:23).

D. The foolish (v. 4). The foolish kill and destroy. They have no kindness or gentle feelings. See Romans 1:25–32.

Abigail was a peacemaker. Jesus told us to be peacemakers (Matt. 5:9). With so much confusion and trouble in the world, God is seeking more peacemakers. Mature Christians should be peacemakers. Always avoid trouble. Try to prevent trouble. Most of our problems are the result of misunderstanding. Be sure to get all the facts, then there will be fewer problems.

31

Nathan, the Bold Prophet

2 Samuel 11:1–27; 12:1–7, 9, 13–14

Nathan was an Old Testament prophet. God used Nathan to expose the sin of David. The king had the power to destroy anyone who disagreed with him. Nathan knew this, but didn't fear, because God had sent him. He knew truth was more important than his personal safety. God used Nathan three times in the life of David: (1) Concerning the temple (2 Sam. 7:1–17); (2) Help in overcoming Adonijah (1 Kings 1:5–53); (3) Exposing David's sin (2 Sam. 12:1–17).

I. The Results of Sin (11:1–27)

A. Sin (11:1–25). David commits adultery (11:1–5). He has Uriah, the husband of Bathsheba, killed in battle (11:15–17).

B. Sorrow (11:26–27a). Uriah is dead. Bathsheba mourns for him. David marries Bathsheba. She is expecting his child (11:5).

C. Shame (11:27b). What David did displeased the Lord. Sin always brings sorrow. See Proverbs 13:15.

II. The Revealing of Sin (12:1–7, 9)

A. Study (vv. 1–6). Parable of a rich man taking a lamb from a poor man. David is angry—this man would pay for his sin four-fold. Note v. 7a, "Thou art the man."

B. Shame (v. 7, 9). God anointed David king. He was delivered from Saul. Why did David sin? He wasn't living in the Spirit. See Galatians 5:16.

III. The Repentance of Sin (12:13a)

A. Confession to God—"I have sinned against the Lord."

B. Calling to God (Ps. 51:2, 7, 10, 12)

1. Cleansing (v. 2). Cleanse me from sin.
2. Washing (v. 7). Make me whiter than snow.
3. Creation (v. 10). Create a clean heart in me.
4. Restoration (vv. 12–13a). Restore unto me the joy of the Lord.

IV. The Remission from Sin (12:13b)

A. Pardon—"The Lord also hath put away thy sin." Confession of sin is necessary (Ps. 51:17). If one confesses sin, God will forgive (1 John 1:9).

B. Promise—"Thou shalt not die." Note the promise of John 5:24, how one passes from death unto life.

V. The Regret of Sin (12:14)

A. Sin (14a). David's sin left a very bad example. Keep in mind, David was a man after God's heart (1 Sam. 13:14). God was looking at David's heart when he chose him. Compare with 1 Samuel 16:7. David sinned by his own choice.

B. Suffering (14b). The child of Bathsheba would die. David would reap what he sowed. Note Galatians 6:7, 8. Regardless of whom the person may be, one reaps what one sows—good or bad!

Because Nathan obeyed God, David was brought back to God. One must be willing to obey God, even if he or she stands alone! When one is sent to show and expose sin, it should be done in a kind and loving way. It must be done in love, concern, and compassion. Compare with James 5:17, 20. Be willing to be used of God to bring others back to Christ. And remember, even strong Christians can fall into sin, if they are not careful how they live.

32

Wisdom, Wealth, Wonder

1 Kings 3:16–22, 24–28; 4:20–34

Solomon requested wisdom from God; God granted him his request. James says that if we need wisdom, we should ask God, and he will give it (James 1:5). Now we see this wisdom tested. God not only gave Solomon wisdom, he also gave him wealth. God gives people certain talents and gifts. He expects these to be used bringing glory unto God.

I. The Wisdom of Solomon (3:16–22, 24–28)

A. Problem (vv. 16–22). Two harlots had babies. One baby died. The mother of the dead baby exchanges her baby with the baby of the other mother while she slept. Solomon had a hard decision to make. (1) Both women had poor character. (2) There were no witnesses. (3) Questioning brought only denials.

B. Plan (vv. 24–25). Solomon asks the baby be cut in half, giving half to each woman.

C. Pity (vv. 26–27). The real mother could not remain silent. She didn't want her son killed. Verse 27 reveals the real mother.

D. Power (v. 28). All Israel heard of Solomon's wisdom. They knew God was with him.

II. The Wealth of Solomon (4:20–23, 25–27)

A. Promise (vv. 20, 25). God brought blessing to Solomon and joy to the nation. God wants his people happy. Note this joy:

1. Full of joy in his presence (Ps. 16:11).
2. Christ's joy being in us (John 15:11).
3. Having joy in the Lord (John 17:13).

4. Sow in tears, reaping in joy (Ps. 126:5).
5. Asking that our joy may be full (John 16:24).

B. Prosperity (vv. 21–23, 26–27). Solomon had much wealth. God does promise to meet all our needs (Phil. 4:19; Ps. 37:25). When you pray, don't ask for selfish reasons, ask for the glory of God. Compare with Luke 12:15.

III. The Wonder of Solomon (4:29–34)

A. Personal wisdom (v. 29). Solomon said, "Happy is the man that findeth wisdom" (Prov. 3:13). He knew happiness was not in riches, but in knowing God.

B. Powerful wisdom (vv. 30–31). People and leaders respect Solomon for his wisdom. Note again James 1:5. One of the gifts of the Spirit is the word of wisdom (1 Cor. 12:8).

C. Proverbs with wisdom (vv. 32–33). Solomon passed his wisdom on to others. Psalms 72 and 127 were written by him, as well as the Song of Solomon.

D. Person and wisdom (v. 34). People came from near and far to see this wise man. All his wisdom was from God.

All Christians should seek wisdom. The Bible encourages us to seek wisdom (James 1:5). God has set in the church spiritual gifts which help the child of God to make wise decisions. They are: the word of wisdom, the word of knowledge, and discerning spirits. The child of God needs these gifts to help him solve problems, as well as know the truth.

33

The Queen of Sheba Visits Solomon

1 Kings 10:1–13

Solomon was the richest man who ever lived. The Queen of Sheba came for a visit. Though Solomon was great, the queen was more impressed with the God he served. The lives of God's people should bring honor and glory to God. People shouldn't look at what we have done but rather what God has done through us. Solomon was interested in giving glory to God (1 Kings 8:41–42).

I. The Request of the Queen (vv. 1–2)

A. Godliness (v. 1). The queen was impressed. Solomon's early life was a great testimony to God (1 Kings 10:1). His life left an impact on the entire world.

B. Giving (v. 2). When the queen came, she was prepared. She brought riches. When we come to the Lord, we must come prepared. See Psalm 100:4.

C. Gifts. Gifts we give unto the Lord: time, talent, money, life. When God has control of these, our lives will bless all people we come in contact with daily.

II. The Revelation to the Queen (vv. 3–5)

A. Interest (v. 3). The queen asks many questions. A wise answer was given by Solomon for each question asked. Keep in mind, all this wisdom was divine wisdom! See James 1:5.

B. Influence (v. 4). "She soon realized that everything she ever heard about his great wisdom was true. She also saw the beautiful palace he had built" (LB).

C. Impact (v. 5). Solomon was more impressive than the queen had heard, or had expected. His kingdom was great, but it was God who gave his greatness. Note that without God, we are nothing (John 15:5). With him, we are powerful (Phil. 4:13). We may read of God's kingdom and hear of its beauty, but we cannot fully understand its beauty and glory (1 Cor. 2:9).

III. The Results and the Queen (vv. 6–13)

A. Seeing (vv. 6–7). The queen said if she had not seen, she would not have believed. The Bible teaches we must believe before we see (Heb. 11:1, 6; Rom. 10:17).

B. Satisfaction (v. 8). We serve one greater than Solomon! We serve Jesus Christ! His name is above all names (Phil. 2:9–11).

C. Selection (v. 9). Praise to God who set Solomon up as king. Praise because he gives justice.

D. Sharing (vv. 10–13).

1. Queen's gifts (vv. 10–12). *The Living Bible* says the queen gave Solomon the equivalent of about $3,500,000 in gold plus other gifts.
2. Solomon's gifts (v. 13). Solomon gave her many gifts. She was given whatever she desired.

The Queen of Sheba heard of Solomon's glory. She was not disappointed. She was deeply impressed. As we read God's Word, we will be impressed with God's promises of heaven and its glory. Solomon said, "The half has not yet been told." God created the beauties of heaven and earth in six days. He is now preparing a place for his people. No one can describe such a place.

34

Elijah Raises the Dead

1 Kings 17:1–24

Elijah was called by God to do his work. He was very bold! He was a fearless prophet: fearless as he appears before king Ahab; fearless as he asks the widow for the last meal; fearless as he promises the widow her supply of food would last indefinitely; fearless as he prays for life to return to the widow's dead son. God works through fearless people.

I. The Personality of Elijah (vv. 1–7)

A. The prophet (v. 1). Elijah appears before King Ahab, saying it would not rain for several years. It was God who sent Elijah. Note how God calls and sends man (John 1:6).

B. The plan (vv. 2–5).

1. The call (vv. 2–4). Elijah is told by God to go to a secret brook of Cherith. Compare with Matthew 6:6.
2. The consecration (v. 5). Elijah obeys the voice of God.

C. The provision (v. 6). The ravens bring Elijah bread and meat and he drinks from the brook. Compare with Psalm 37:25.

D. The problem (v. 7). The brook dries up. All must be taken from us at times to depend on God. Compare with John 15:5.

II. The Provision for Elijah (vv. 8–16)

A. Plan (vv. 8–9). Elijah is told to go to Zarephath and that widow would take care of him. Compare with Philippians 4:19.

B. Provision (vv. 10–12). The widow has enough food for one small meal. She would prepare this for her and her son, then wait to die by starvation. Now Elijah asks her for food!

C. Promise (vv. 13–15). Elijah promised the widow that her provisions would not fail. The widow obeys. Note how she ate for many days. Give and God gives in return (Luke 6:38).
D. Power (v. 16). She and her family had plenty to eat. See again Philippians 4:19.

III. The Power of Elijah (vv. 17–24)
A. Problem (v. 17). The widow's son dies. Death comes to all regardless of their age (Heb. 9:27).
B. Probing (v. 18). The widow thought God was punishing her for something in her life.
C. Power (vv. 19–22). Elijah takes the dead son, breathes into him, and life returns.
D. Prophet (vv. 23–24). The widow says, "Now by this I know that thou art a man of God." The power of God in Elijah's life showed the power of God. Compare with the testimony Peter and John leave (Acts 4:13).

God provides for all of our needs when we serve and follow him. Sometimes people want things that hurt their relationship with God. God does not answer this prayer. Every person has different needs. The all-wise God knows about these and will meet them accordingly. At all times when you pray, seek God's will (1 John 5:14).

35

Ahab's Covetousness

1 Kings 21:1–4, 7–8, 11–29

God sent Elijah to rebuke Ahab. Elijah is very bold. The sin of coveting causes Ahab to commit murder. The Ten Commandments warn us not to covet (Exod. 20:17). Note these two things about coveting: (1) God hates coveting (Ps. 10:3); (2) coveting will keep you out of heaven (1 Cor. 6:10). Coveting led Jezebel, Ahab's wife, to have Naboth murdered. Coveting always leads to worse sins.

I. The Problem of Ahab (vv. 1–4)

A. Request (vv. 1–2). Ahab wanted Naboth's vineyard; Ahab's heart was on selfish gain. Riches do not satisfy. Note the words of Solomon (Eccles. 5:10).

B. Rejection (v. 3). Naboth could not sell the vineyard, since the Jewish law forbade this (Lev. 25:23–28; Num. 36:7–9).

C. Result (v. 4). Ahab acted childishly. He refused to eat. He was so immature. It's important to be content with what we have (1 Tim. 6:6–8; Phil. 4:11). Note the evils of loving money (1 Tim. 6:10). Money is not evil—"the love of money is the root of all evil."

II. The Plan of Ahab (vv. 7–8, 11–16)

A. Promise (v. 7). Jezebel promises her husband Ahab he would have the vineyard. Through deceit, she would get it.

B. Plan (vv. 8, 11–13). Two people were told to lie about Naboth saying he blasphemed God, and the king. Naboth was put to death. Who was responsible for this?

1. False witnesses. People will believe a lie before they believe the truth.
2. Naboth's enemies. They were fearful of Jezebel. Others perhaps didn't care about truth or justice.

C. Problem (vv. 14–16). Jezebel sent a letter, telling the men to kill Naboth. This wicked woman would meet death in a terrible way. See 2 Kings 9:10, 36.

III. The Prediction to Ahab (vv. 17–24)

A. Sin (vv. 17–19). God speaks through Elijah, revealing Ahab's and Jezebel's sin. God would send judgment on them.

B. Shame (v. 20). Note: "Because thou hast sold thyself to work evil in the sight of the Lord."

C. Sorrow (vv. 21–24). Look at the coming judgment of Jezebel (2 Kings 9:10, 36.) What you sow, you must reap (Gal. 6:7–8).

IV. The Pity Toward Ahab (vv. 25–29)

A. Confession (vv. 25–27). Much of Ahab's wickedness was the result of his wife's influence.

B. Compassion (vv. 28–29). Sometimes God holds back judgment if a person truly repents.

A dissatisfied person will covet. Happiness means satisfaction in what a person has. A coveting person is unhappy; he is never satisfied. Solomon was the richest man who ever lived, yet he was unhappy. See Ecclesiastes 12:1. Unless God is first in life, there will be unhappiness. There will be coveting. This coveting will lead to other sins.

36

Elisha Raises the Dead

2 Kings 4:18–22, 25–27, 30, 32–36

Death is an enemy all of us must face. Unless the Lord returns, all will die. Christ may come before we die, but then it could be years before he returns. Christ overcame death. Because he overcame, we too shall live eternally (John 11:25, 26). For the Christian, death is the start of eternal life. God used Elisha to bring life to a dead man. He can use us to bring spiritual life to the sinner.

I. The Power of Death (vv. 18–21)

A. Sickness (vv. 18–19). A child, perhaps five to seven years old, had died. Death at times comes even to children.

B. Sorrow (v. 20). Despite all the love of the mother, the child died. Death is sure (Heb. 9:27).

C. Sincere (v. 21). The son was promised by Elisha (vv. 14–17). No doubt there was faith in Elisha that he could raise the dead child. Death is sudden (Prov. 27:1). Each year in America 45,000 or more die in auto accidents. Many thousands die in other accidents or from sudden sickness. No one has power over death, except Christ.

II. The Power in Death (vv. 22, 25, 27–30)

A. Confidence (v. 22). The woman calls for the man of God. She knew Elisha was a man of God (v. 9). A man of God is someone who walks and talks with God daily.

B. Concern (vv. 25–27). Elisha was interested in the needs of the woman. Living near God creates a concern for the needs of others. Compare with Galatians 6:1, 2.

C. Constrained (vv. 28–30). This woman would not give up. Elisha didn't come immediately. The woman kept after him. She was determined. See Luke 11:5–8. Those who receive things from God are those who don't quit or give up easily.

III. The Power over Death (vv. 32–36)

A. The prayer (vv. 32–34). Elisha closes the door and prays to God in secret. Secret prayer is important (Matt. 6:6). See the words of Isaiah 40:31. Note two important things about Elisha's prayer: (1) simple prayer—he didn't try to impress others; (2) sincere prayer—he prayed from his heart unto God.

B. The power (vv. 35–36). The child is restored to life. It was God's power working through Elisha. God gives life.

1. He gives enjoyable life (John 10:10).
2. He gives exciting life (Ps. 16:11).
3. He gives eternal life (John 5:24).

The Shunammite woman had great faith in God. Even though her son died, that didn't weaken her faith. Sorrow, disappointment and problems should strengthen our faith—not weaken it! How we react during these times will depend much on our faith. Anyone can have faith when all things are going well. God can give us the faith that will not weaken under problems, faith that will expect God to do the impossible.

37

Naaman, the Obedient Captain

2 Kings 5:1–14

Naaman's sin was pride! This sin keeps people from accepting the Lord. This sin keeps Christians from having God's best! All pride, whether in the Christian or sinner is sin! It displeases God, it is pride that keeps people from seeing their need of God. It causes people to feel they can do all things by themselves.

I. The Sickness of Naaman (v. 1).

A. Person—"Now Naaman, captain of the host of the king of Syria, was a great man with his master, and honourable, because by him the LORD had given deliverance to Syria."

B. Power—"He was also a mighty man in valour." He was respected by the people.

C. Problem—"But he was a leper." Leprosy:

1. Cannot be hidden (Num. 32:23).
2. Can be cured by God only (1 John 1:9; John 14:6).
3. Is unclean (Jer. 17:9).
4. Spreads quickly (Rom. 3:23). All people have this sickness of sin (Rom. 3:10; Isa. 53:6).

II. The Servant of Naaman (vv. 2–6)

A. Humility (v. 2). A small maid who served Naaman's wife.

B. Hope (v. 3). There was hope for Naaman and his sickness if he saw Elisha. Our hope is in Christ (Acts 4:12)

C. Help (vv. 4–5). The small maid was told to take the message of hope and help to Naaman. We have a message to share. See Mark 16:15; John 16:15.

D. Healing (v. 6). The small maid brought a simple message of healing. God's plan of health is given in Exodus 15:26.

III. The Stubbornness of Naaman (vv. 7–13)

A. Problem (v. 7). Naaman becomes angry. Often when God speaks, conviction makes man angry.

B. Prophecy (vv. 8–9). Elisha invites Naaman to visit him. He accepts. Obedience is necessary to come to God to receive anything from him.

C. Plan (v. 10). Elisha tells Naaman to take seven dips in the muddy Jordan. The key to success is obedience (John 14:15).

D. Pride (vv. 11–12). Naaman was too proud to take a dip in the muddy water. Pride separates us from God (James 4:6).

E. People (v. 13). Naaman's servants encourage him to obey the words of the prophet. (Note 1 Sam. 15:22)

IV. The Submission of Naaman (v. 14).

A. Pride/pride aside. Note: "Then he went down, and dipped himself seven times in the Jordan." Humility brings God's blessings.

B. Prophet. "According to the saying of the man of God."

C. Perfection. "And his flesh came again like unto the flesh of a little child, and he was clean."

Pride almost kept Naaman from receiving his healing. Pride always separates us from God. Humility is something we must practice daily. Paul said, "Not I, but Christ liveth in me" (Gal. 2:20). Selfish ambitions and pride destroy humility. Jesus taught how he must be first in our lives (Matt. 6:33).

38

Ezra's God-given Mission

Ezra 7:6–10, 27–28, 8:15, 21–23

How often in Israel's history people wandered from God. God would bless them and meet their needs. They soon would forget him. In this passage we see Ezra leading Israel from captivity in Babylon to Jerusalem. History records that there seems to be no hope, and when sin seems to abound, God always has a plan and person to do his work. God found in Ezra a man he could trust and use.

I. The Instruction of the Leader (7:6–10)

A. Desire (v. 6).

1. Student. *The Living Bible* says Ezra was "well versed in Jehovah's law." He was a student of God's Word. See 2 Timothy 2:15.
2. Spiritual. Ezra requests permission to return to Jerusalem. *The Living Bible* says, "The Lord his God was blessing him!" He was granted his request. Note our requests (Phil. 4:6).

B. Destination (vv. 7–9). They leave Babylon and travel to Jerusalem. God gave them a good trip. He is with us (Matt. 28:20). He guides us if we permit him (Prov. 3:5, 6).

C. Determination (v. 10). Ezra was determined to know God's Word. In *The Living Bible*, v. 10, it says he was determined to study, obey and become a Bible teacher. He became one of the Jewish scribes. What an ambition to study God's Word. See Psalm 119:11; 1 Peter 3:15. Jesus' last sermon was to teach all nations (Matt. 28:19).

II. The Influence of the Leader (7:27–28)

A. The past (v. 27). "Well, praise the Lord God of our ancestors, who made the king want to beautify the Temple of the

Lord in Jerusalem!" (LB) The King of Persia, Artaxerzes, gave permission. Ezra was given authority over the Jewish settlements east of the Euphrates.

B. The present (v. 28). God gave Ezra special wisdom and directions. We are told to ask for wisdom (James 1:5). Ezra gives praise to God for all the accomplishments.

III. The Inspiration of the Leader (8:15, 21–23)

A. Problem (v. 15). No one volunteered to assist Ezra in the work of God. God still seeks man to do his work. See Ezekiel 22:30. Compare with David's complaint in Psalm 124:4.

B. Plan (v. 21). Ezra has a plan—to fast! He desired that the people be humble before God. Compare with 2 Chronicles 7:14. God protected them as they traveled. Compare with Psalm 91:4.

C. Provision (v. 22). Ezra didn't depend on human power and strength. "Some trust in chariots, and some in horses: but we will remember the name of the Lord our God" (Ps. 20:7).

D. Protection (v. 23). "So we fasted and begged God to take care of us. And he did" (LB). He cares about us (Heb. 4:15).

Ezra could have taken the attitude, "What's the use—all hope is gone!" But he looked beyond the problem and saw a God who performs miracles when he finds the people to work through. Ezra not only knew about God—he also knew God personally. He knew God's Word. He knew God's will and God's way for himself and God's people.

39

Nehemiah—God's Worker

Nehemiah 1:4; 2:18–20; 4:6, 18, 20, 23; 6:3

Nehemiah was the cupbearer of the king. God called him to rebuild the broken-down walls of Jerusalem. As God called him, so he calls Christians to build up his work today. We have a breakdown of our homes, a breakdown of morality, and indifference among Christians. We need those who will rebuild.

I. The Feeling of Nehemiah (1:4)

A. A passionate feeling—he wept!
   1. Jeremiah wept over the lost (Jer. 9:1).
   2. The psalmist tells of weeping (Ps. 126:5).
   3. Look how Jesus wept over the lost (John 1:35).
   4. Paul wept over the lost (Acts 20:31).

B. A personal feeling—he mourned! He felt a need to mourn for the sins of the nation and mourn for the shortcomings of Christianity. Look at Moses' mourning (Exod. 32:32).

C. A prayer of fervency—he wept! To accomplish some things, there must be fasting. See Mark 9:29.

II. The Faith of Nehemiah (2:18–20)

A. Surrender—"Let us rise up and build." Full surrender to God causes us to work for him. Compare with Acts 9:6.

B. Strength—"They strengthened their hands." Faith in Christ will strengthen us to do God's work. Note that faith is necessary to please God (Heb. 11:6). Note the great people of faith in Hebrews 11.

C. Soundness (2:19). The enemies could not hinder Nehemiah's work. There will always be opposition, but God is on our side. See Romans 8:31; Isaiah 54:17.

D. Surety (2:20). God in heaven prospered them. As we seek God, he gives prosperity. See 2 Chronicles 26:5.

III. The Fervency of Nehemiah (4:6; 18, 20, 23)

A. Faithfulness (vv. 6, 18). They worked with one hand and held a sword in the other. They protected what they had. See Revelation 3:11. Then note Ecclesiastes 9:10.

B. Faith (v. 20). God will fight for us. He is on our side and will help us. See Exodus 14:13, 14.

C. Fervency (v. 23). They were willing to work overtime. God sees and will reward (Mal. 3:16).

IV. The Firmness of Nehemiah (6:3)

A. "I am doing a great work so that I cannot come down." He was too busy to complain. Christians should not complain.

B. He was too busy to criticize. Note the warning of criticism by Jesus (Matt. 7:1–5).

C. He was too busy to compromise. Never allow opinions to replace God's Word. See Revelation 22:18.

Every person has a place in God's work. We can and must build the work of God. Having an indifferent attitude hinders God's work. Satan has always hindered God's work. He blinds people to the truth of God's Word (2 Cor. 4:4). As Christians work together, God's work will go forward.

40

Esther's Dedicated Service

Esther 2:8–20

Esther was a simple Jewish girl who became a queen. This was not an accident. God's hand was on her. Through cooperation and dedication God could trust and use her. Some people pray, "Use me." We should pray, "Make me usable." If we are usable, God will use us. The attitude of Esther is an excellent example for us to follow.

I. Esther's Preparation (vv. 8–14)

A. Plan (v. 8). The king of Persia, Ahasuerus, wants Queen Vashti to come to a lascivious banquet, but she refuses. The queen is banished. Esther is brought into the court of Anasuerus, to the place where she could be used of God. See Psalm 37:23.

B. Preparation (vv. 9–14).

1. Pleasure (v. 9). Esther pleased the king. As a result she received special kindness.
2. Person (vv. 10–11). Esther was a Jewess. Mordecai told her to keep this a secret.
3. Preparation (v. 12–14). Special beauty treatments were given to Esther. The Bible does not approve of the action of vv. 13–14. This was the custom of the day!

II. Esther's Presentation (vv. 15–16)

A. Pleasure (v. 15). Esther was beautiful. She was admired by those in competition with her. She not only had outward beauty—she also had inner beauty. Note how Stephen showed this beauty (Acts 6:15). People saw Christ in the lives of Peter and John (Acts 4:13).

B. Presentation (v. 16). Esther is taken to the king's palace. God's plan would prevail. God in us is greater than the evil one in the world (1 John 4:4). Compare with Romans 8:31.

III. Esther's Promotion (vv. 17–20)

A. Promotion (vv. 17–18). Esther is made queen. She is chosen over others. One may be popular without lowering standards and convictions. Daniel was popular but was righteous (Dan. 1:8–15). God stood with Daniel.

B. Personality (vv. 19–20). Esther is now queen. This did not make her proud. She is still humble and obedient to her cousin and foster father, Mordecai.

C. Plan. Mordecai accepted the job as a gate keeper. It was a humble job. While on duty, he overheard the plan to have the king killed. He spread the word to Esther and the king's life was saved.

God can take a "nobody" and with his help and guidance make a "somebody" in his work. Mordecai and Esther were both simple and submissive to God's will and plan. At first both were unknown, but later would become popular at that time as well as in history. God looks for available people. It does not take great people to do great things—it only takes consecrated people. Esther was available and consecrated and God used her.

41

Esther's Dedication Brings Victory

Esther 7:3–10; 8:1–2

God placed Esther and Mordecai in special places of leadership. They would affect the lives of many Jews. Mordecai refuses to bow before Ashasuerus. He knew the Ten Commandments forbade this (Exod. 20:1–5). The king's assistant was Haman. This assistant seeks to destroy Mordecai. Sinful men always oppose God-fearing people. God who lives in the Christian offends the evil one, Satan, who lives in the sinner. When the Christian and sinner come into contact with each other, there will be friction.

I. The Sinful Plan (7:3–10)

A. Haman's desire (vv. 3–6). Haman wanted to destroy the Jewish race. He planned to start with Mordecai. Esther is told of this plan.

B. Haman's design (vv. 7–10). Haman has a gallows made to hang Mordecai. The king is angry. He orders that Haman be hanged on the gallows he made for Mordecai. Haman reaps what he sows. See Galatians 6:7; Romans 6:23.

C. Haman's destruction. Haman's plan backfires! Someone has said "Don't dig a grave for another person—you may fall into it." God cares for his people. Note the promise from Isaiah 54:17. Moses allowed God to fight for him (Exod. 14:13). Compare with Romans 8:31.

II. The Sincere Praise (8:1–2)

A. Revelation (v. 1). Esther tells the king of her cousin and foster father, Mordecai. The king didn't know that both Esther and Mordecai were Jewish. God chose Esther and

Mordecai to preserve the Jewish race. From this nation would come Christ, the Messiah. See Isaiah 7:14; 9:6.

B. Reward (v. 2). The king gives his ring to Mordecai. This would give Mordecai power. He would be next to the king. He was given the royal apparel. The people of Shushan rejoice (8:15). Mordecai was willing to serve in a humble place. As the result he was promoted.

C. Response. Responding to God plus faithfulness will bring a response from God. See Galatians 6:9. God expects faithfulness. Compare with Revelation 2:10.

III. The Secured People (8:3–12)

A. Request (vv. 3–8). Esther asks for the cancellation of the law which Haman made before he was hanged. She made no demands. She seeks no mercy. We should not seek justice from God—if so, we would be sent to hell. We should seek mercy. Compare with Romans 3:23; 6:23.

B. Response (vv. 9–12). The law Haman made was changed. The Jews were not killed. The prophet says the soul that sins shall die (Ezek. 18:4). The New Testament says if we believe, we shall have life (John 5:24).

What if Esther and Mordecai refused to obey God? God's work would have suffered at this time. When there is a lack of cooperation, his work suffers and is hindered. Mordecai started with a small job and was faithful. If one cannot be faithful in a small job in a small place, how can he be faithful with a large responsibility?

42

The Commitment of Job

Job 1

We often hear of "the patience of Job." Job was patient because of his commitment unto God. He was the richest man living at that time. Job lived at the time of Abraham. Job lost his riches, ten children, and his health. Despite all this, he could still serve God. Note how God permitted Satan to test Job (1:7–12; 2:1–6). We will see how Job came through it all victoriously.

I. The Confidence of Job (1:21, 22)

A. Substance (v. 21). The Lord gave and the Lord took away. See Romans 8:28 and God's plan and purpose.

B. Stability (v. 22). "In all this, Job did not sin or revile God" (LB). We must trust God (Heb. 11:6).

II. The Control of Job (2:9, 10)

A. Suggestion (v. 9). Job's wife asks Job why he would serve God when he loses all. Why not curse God and die? We follow God for what we can *give*—not what we *get*. See John 6:66.

B. Stability (v. 10). Job said in simple words, "I will praise the Lord and live." God was first in Job's life. Compare with Matthew 6:33.

III. The Chastening of Job (5:17)

A. The practice of chastening. "Behold, happy is the man whom God correcteth [disciplines]." Those God loves, he chastens (Heb. 12:6).

B. The patience in chastening. "Therefore despise not thou the chastening of the Almighty." We should endure God's chastening (Heb. 12:7).

IV. The Consecration of Job (13:15)

A. Possibility—"Though he slay me." God has the power to give or take life. Compare with Deuteronomy 32:4.

B. Patience—"Yet will I trust him." People must fully place their trust in God (Prov. 3:5, 6). We do not look at circumstances—we look at God.

V. The Commitment of Job (19:25, 26)

A. Faithfulness (v. 25). God is alive. Because he lives, we too shall live. We have the promise of eternal life (John 3:16; 11:25, 26).

B. Faith (v. 26). The body will decay, but the soul shall live forever (John 5:24).

VI. The Completeness of Job (23:10)

A. Respect (v. 23a). God knows and understands our problems. He is touched with our feelings (Heb. 4:15).

B. Reward (v. 23b). After Job was tested, he would come forth as silver. Compare with Psalm 66:10.

Through all his loss and suffering, Job was patient. In the end, God healed him. God restored his loss. He had twice as much as before (Job 42:10, 12). It was Job's commitment that caused him to endure loss and sickness. At times God does heal. He does remove the problems. Sometimes he doesn't. Note 2 Corinthians 12:7–10. God didn't remove Paul's thorn, but was with him during his weakness.

43

The Call of Isaiah

Isaiah 6:1–13

Isaiah had a three-fold vision: (1) He looked *up*—and saw God! (2) He looked *in*—and saw himself. (3) He looked *out*—and saw others. We need this three-fold vision. God will reveal himself if we seek him. Many Christians don't live close enough to God for him to speak to them.

I. The Worship of Isaiah (vv.1–4)

A. Sacred (v. 1). After Uzziah died, Isaiah had a vision of the Lord. No doubt Isaiah was depending on Uzziah—not God! Uzziah now is gone and Isaiah seeks God. Compare with John 15:5.

B. Seraphim (v. 2). This angel had six wings. God's presence was so holy, the seraphim hid his eyes. God is holy (Lev. 19:2).

C. Sinless (v. 3). Note these words, "Holy, Holy, Holy; the whole earth is filled with his glory." We need holiness (Heb. 12:14).

D. Singing (v. 4). "Such singing it was. It shook the Temple to its foundations, and suddenly the entire sanctuary was filled with smoke" (LB).

II. The Woe of Isaiah (vv. 5–7)

A. Confession (v. 5). Note three things in this verse:

1. Undone. He saw his shortcomings.
2. Unclean—having unclean lips.
3. Unfit—saw the Lord. Isaiah saw he was unfit for heaven. Only those living according to God's rules will be in heaven.

B. Cleansing (vv. 6–7). The seraphim flew with fire from heaven and placed it on Isaiah's lips. It cleanses his life. The blood of Christ cleanses (1 John 1:7).

III. The Work for Isaiah (vv. 8–10)

A. Call (v. 8). God calls, "Whom shall I send, and who will go for us?" Isaiah responds, "Here am I, send me." He didn't say, "I can't do it" or "Others are more qualified." He simply said, "Send me." Compare with Matthew 4:19.

B. Confusion (vv. 9–10). The people would hear but not understand. Many people are blind to the truth (2 Cor. 4:4). Others don't understand because they don't want to understand. When people are sincere, God will help them understand.

IV. The Wonder of Isaiah (vv. 11–13)

A. Problem (vv. 11–12). The people would not listen to God's warning about the coming judgment. Very few will listen about the impending judgment of Revelation 10:11–15.

B. Patience (v. 13). All God asks of us is to be faithful. Sow the seed—God will bring the results. Don't give up (Gal. 6:9). Not all people listened to Jesus and his teaching when he was on earth.

Before God can use you, there must be a personal relationship with him. Before we can touch others we must be touched by God! This touch need not be a dream or a vision—just a daily personal relationship with God. As people have this personal relationship with God, he will use them. He will direct them. Isaiah was a normal person, but God used Isaiah because he permitted God to touch him.

44

Hezekiah's Life Extended

Isaiah 38:1–5

This passage is similar to 2 Kings 18–20; 2 Chronicles 29–32. In these verses we see Hezekiah being told he would die, his sorrow about the impending death, and his prayer for extended life. God saw his repentance and sorrow. God heard his prayer. He added fifteen years to Hezekiah's life. Only God can lengthen life. The extended life was for a purpose—to glorify God.

I. The Pronouncement (v. 1)

A. Problem (v. 1a). Hezekiah was sick. The sickness was a boil. See v. 21. The prophet visits him. Hezekiah was the fourteenth king of Judah. He was the father of Manasseh.

B. Pronouncement (v. 1b). "Set your affairs in order, for you are going to die; you will not recover from this illness" (LB).

1. The Christian's death (2 Cor. 5:8). Separation from the body, soul with the Lord. Christians dwell in the house of the Lord forever (Ps. 23:6). See also 2 Cor. 5:1.
2. The sinner's death (Heb. 9:27). All must die (Eccles. 3:2). After death comes the judgment of Revelation 20:11–15.

C. Promise (John 5:24). Accepting Christ causes us to pass from death to life. Compare with Jesus' words of John 14:19.

II. The Prayer (vv. 2–3)

A. Report (v. 2). "When Hezekiah heard this, he turned his face to the wall and prayed" (LB). Though he was ready to die, he wanted to live longer to work for God.

B. Reminder (v. 3a). Hezekiah reminds God of three important things:
   1. I have walked before you in truth.
   2. I have walked before you with a perfect heart.
   3. I have done that which is good in your sight.

   He didn't understand why this would happen to him. All God's people must remember Romans 8:28. See also Isaiah 55:8, 9. Also God's will must always be considered.
C. Remorse (v. 3b). "Then he broke down with great sobs" (LB). Compare with 2 Kings 20:3.

III. The Promise (vv. 4–5)

A. Announcement (v. 4). The prophet is sent again to Hezekiah with a different message. God saw his sincere heart, and answered his prayer.
B. Answer (v. 5a). God does hear our prayers. Note the promise of Jeremiah 33:3. Of course, it is important to pray according to God's will (1 John 5:14, 15). And keep in mind that God always answers prayer in three ways: Yes, No, Wait. His answers are for our good though we may not see it immediately.
C. Addition (v. 5b). God added fifteen years of Hezekiah's life. He died after reigning for twenty-nine years. This is the only person God told how long he would live.

Hezekiah's life was extended for the glory of God. We should always remember the length of life is not as important as the content. If God's people use their time wisely each day, they will have a life pleasing unto God. This will be a life that is successful regardless of the length of it. God has the right to lengthen or shorten our life. We don't know the length of life, therefore we should be concerned with how we live.

45

Jeremiah—the Fearless Prophet

Jeremiah 1:4–8, 19; 26:2–9, 12–16

God has always called people to do his work. When God called Jeremiah, he responded by saying he couldn't speak because he was a child (Jer. 1:6). God took this young man and made him a fearless prophet. The God who called him, gave him the strength to fulfill this call. Jeremiah chose the hard way because of God's call.

I. The Personality of Jeremiah (1:4–6)

A. God's plan (vv. 4–5). God said these things to Jeremiah: before you were born, I knew thee; I formed thee; I sanctified thee; I ordained thee.

B. God's provision (v. 6). "'O Lord God,' I said, 'I can't do that! I'm far too young! I'm only a youth.'" (LB). When God calls someone, he equips (Matt. 4:19).

II. The Promises to Jeremiah (1:7–8, 19)

A. Promise (v. 7). "'Don't say that,' he replied, 'for you will go wherever I send you and speak whatever I tell you to.'" (LB).

B. Provision (v. 8). "'And don't be afraid of the people, for I, the Lord, will be with you and see you through.'" (LB)

C. Power (v. 19). Man can hurt, but God will deliver. Compare with Isaiah 59:19.

III. The Preaching of Jeremiah (26:1–7)

A. Preaching (vv. 1–2). Jeremiah would stand in the Lord's court and preach to those coming to the temple.

B. Plan (vv. 3–6). If the people hear and repent, God will forgive. See 1 John 1:9. If we do not repent, judgment will fall.

C. People (v. 7). The priests, prophets, and people hear these words. They were living ungodly lives.

IV. The Persecution of Jeremiah (26:8, 9)

A. Persecution (v. 8). The people capture Jeremiah and plan to kill him. God's people always suffer (2 Tim. 3:12). See also Matthew 5:10–12.

B. Prophecy (v. 9). Jeremiah's message was "Destruction is coming!" The people didn't like this message. Destruction of the Temple meant the center of worship would be destroyed. Note the previous warning of Jeremiah in Jeremiah 11:21.

V. The Protection of Jeremiah (26:12–16)

A. Prophecy (vv. 12–13). He spoke what God told him. Paul tells how some people wouldn't want truth (2 Tim. 4:3–4).

B. Plea (vv. 14–15). If they wanted to kill Jeremiah, go ahead, but judgment would fall.

C. Peace (v. 16). Quickly the enemies made peace with Jeremiah. Jeremiah would not die. Note the earlier promise (1:8, 19).

Jeremiah suffered much for God. Note the following references: 28:13; 32:2, 3; 33:1; 37:15; 39:15–18. He spent much time in prison. He was often called "the weeping prophet." He chose the unpopular way. Following God is unpopular. Note the words of Jesus in Matthew 7:14. Note being partakers in suffering (1 Peter 4:13).

46

Ezekiel—the Watchman

Ezekiel 18:5–19

God has not called the Christian to an easy life. The prophets, apostles, and Christians suffered much for the Lord. Ezekiel was in a very hard place, but God was with him. All dedicated Christians face problems and persecutions (2 Tim. 3:12; John 15:18, 19). It is Satan who persecutes the Christian and hinders the work of God.

I. The Mission of Ezekiel (vv. 5–9)

A. People (vv. 5–6). Ezekiel was sent to God's people, Israel. They had once known God, but now were no longer following his laws.

B. Practice (v. 7). Israel refused to listen to God. Note the warning of those who forget God (Ps. 9:17): (1) impudent—the strong-headed; (2) hardhearted—the stubborn toward God.

C. Power (vv. 8–9). God would strengthen Ezekiel, giving him the needed strength to warn those who forgot God. Note the words of Jesus, giving the disciple encouragement to do his work (Mark 16:15–18). Note the promised strength in Philippians 4:13.

II. The Might of Ezekiel (vv. 10–14)

A. Words (v. 10). God would give Ezekiel the words to warn the people of their sin. He will give power to witness. Note Acts 1:8. Also see the words of Zechariah 4:6.

B. Work (v. 11). Go and speak to the people if they listen or not. Paul says in the last days people will not want to hear the truth (2 Tim. 4:3–4). Ezekiel had a vision. Before working for God, we must have our eyes open. There must be a vision.

1. A vision of God (Isa. 6:1–8).
2. A vision of hell (Luke 6:19–31).
3. A vision of the lost (Prov. 29:18).

III. The Message of Ezekiel (vv. 15–21)

A. Sharing (v. 15). For seven days Ezekiel "sat with the people." He knew how they felt. He knew their problems. He went to where the people were. God is touched with the feelings of our weakness (Heb. 4:15). We need to have the same feeling toward the non-Christians.

B. Solemnity (vv. 16–19).

1. Watchman (vv. 16–17). A watchman warns of coming judgment. We should warn of the judgment of Revelation 20:11–15.
2. Wicked (v. 18). Warn the wicked. If we do not accept Christ we are lost! See John 3:3; Mark 16:16.
3. Warning (v. 19). If you warn the wicked and they reject the warning, you have done your part.

C. Seriousness (vv. 20–21). Be faithful in witnessing.

We have many warning devices which protect our lives. We need to warn people of the coming judgment. God calls human beings to do this warning. He could use angels, but he has called us to carry out this work. People must be shown that they are sinners (Rom. 3:23). They must be warned that the price of sin is death (Rom. 6:23).

47

Daniel's Complete Dedication

Daniel 3:1–30

The three Hebrew boys, Shadrach, Meshach, and Abednego, were willing to stand for God, even if it meant standing against a whole nation. Though it would mean suffering, they were willing to stand for what was right. As they stood for God, he stood with them, giving them strength and courage.

I. The Plan (vv. 1–12)

A. Person (v. 1). Nebuchadnezzar, king of Babylon, made a golden image of himself. It was ninety feet high and nine feet wide.

B. Punishment (vv. 2–7). All the people were asked to bow before the image. Those who refused were to be cast into the fire. See v. 6.

C. Principle (v. 12). These boys knew it was wrong to bow before idols. They knew Exodus 20:1–6.

II. The Problem (vv. 13–18)

A. Anger (vv. 13–15). The king is angry because the boys refuse to bow. He will give them a second chance.

B. Attitude (vv. 16–18).

1. Deliverance (vv. 16–17). God can deliver us from the fire. Compare with Psalm 91.
2. Determination (v. 18). If God doesn't deliver, they were willing to die in the fire. See Acts 20:24.

III. The Punishment (vv. 19–23)

A. Fury (vv. 19–20). The king was very angry because the boys refused to bow to the idol. They were given a second chance, again they refused to bow.

B. Fire (vv. 21–23. The boys were cast into the fire. It was seven times hotter than usual. The guards who put the boys in the fire died.

IV. The Protection (vv. 24–27)

A. Protection (vv. 24–25). There were four men in the fire—only three were thrown in the fire. The fourth one was like the Son of God. He promised never to leave us (Matt. 28:20).

B. Perfection (vv. 26–27). The king calls for the boys to come forth from the fire. Note this: "Then the princes, governors, captains and counselors crowded around them and saw that the fire hadn't touched them—not a hair of their heads was singed; their coats were unscorched, and they didn't even smell of smoke!" (LB) The fourth person remained in the fire so when we go through the fire, he is with us.

V. The Promotion (vv. 28–30)

A. Determination (v. 28). They had great influence on others.

B. Decree (v. 29). Those speaking against these boys were punished.

C. Dedication (v. 30). Dedication brought promotion.

God stands for those who stand for him. At times it may appear we stand alone. These three boys were willing to stand even if it meant to stand alone. Note the words of Jesus, how if we are ashamed of him on earth, he will be ashamed of us in heaven (Mark 8:34–38). At all times, and all circumstances, stand for him!

48

Nebuchadnezzar's Dream

Daniel 4:1–28

God warns Nebuchadnezzar of impending judgment. God always warns before he sends judgment. He warned Adam what would happen if he ate the forbidden fruit (Gen. 2:17). Many people hear his voice but refuse to obey. Note God's judgment comes to those who reject him and his Word (Ps. 9:17; Mark 16:16).

I. The Disposition Displayed (vv. 1–3)

A. Proclamation (v. 1). Nebuchadnezzar sent a message to all people of the earth and of every language.

B. Power (vv. 2–3)

1. Personality (v. 2). The wonders of God were shown unto the king.
2. Power (v. 3). Nebuchadnezzar saw in the dream the greatness of God's power whose kingdom is everlasting.

II. The Dilemma of the Dream (vv. 4–7)

A. Person (v. 4). Nebuchadnezzar was living in prosperity.

B. Problem (v. 5). The dream brought fear to Nebuchadnezzar because he didn't understand it.

C. Powerless (vv. 6–7). The magicians and astrologers, Chaldeans, and soothsayers could not interpret the dream.

III. The Details of the Dream (vv. 8–18)

A. Person (v. 8). Daniel is called before Nebuchadnezzar. He is a holy man. He is called "Belteshazzar," meaning he had power with God. Note our power with God (Phil. 4:13).

B. Particulars (vv. 9–18).

---

1. Tall tree. It grows till all can see (vv. 9–11).
2. Fruit for all people and meat as well (v. 12).
3. An angel comes from heaven (v. 13).
4. Destroying the tree but allowing the stump to remain as well as the roots (vv. 14–15).
5. Nebuchadnezzar driven into the field as an animal (vv. 16–17).
6. The meaning of the dream (v. 18).

IV. The Dream Defined (vv. 19–28)

A. Response (v. 19). Daniel was stunned, not knowing the meaning of the dream nor having power to interpret it.

B. Revelation (vv. 20–26). The meaning of the dream shown to Daniel by the Lord. He gives wisdom. See James 1:5.

1. Tall tree (vv. 20–22). The tall tree was Nebuchadnezzar because he was known worldwide.
2. Angel cutting down the tree (v. 23) meant that Nebuchadnezzar would be taken from his throne.
3. Seven years of animal life (vv. 24–25). Nebuchadnezzar would live as an animal for seven years.
4. Stump and roots (v. 26). God would return his kingdom to Nebuchadnezzar after seven years.

C. Repentance (vv. 27–28). If Nebuchadnezzar repented of his sin, God would perhaps spare him of the coming trouble.

Later judgment falls on Nebuchadnezzar. If we ignore God's warnings, judgments must fall. God is not obligated to warn us, but in his mercy he does.

49

Nebuchadnezzar's Pride, Punishment, Pardon

Daniel 4:29–37

Nebuchadnezzar was a great king. *The Living Bible* says he was a prospered king (Dan. 4:4). He allowed pride to enter his heart. He made the golden image of himself, requiring all his subjects to bow before it (Dan. 3:1). He forgot how God freed the Hebrew boys from the fiery furnace. He forgot the God who gave him all things. He forgot that when one dies all possessions are left behind. He was rich materially but poor spiritually.

I. The Pride of Nebuchadnezzar (vv. 29–32)

A. Forgotten counsel (v. 29). Nebuchadnezzar had a dream of a tree being cut down (Dan. 4:10–18). Daniel interprets the dream, explaining that God would send judgment because Nebuchadnezzar had forgotten God. One year passes before the judgment comes. God is patient toward Nebuchadnezzar, waiting for him to repent.

B. Forgotten conceit (v. 30). Nebuchadnezzar took credit for all his success. He had assistants to help him, but he does not mention them. He was proud and haughty. Note three things about pride:

1. It starts with selfish ambitions and desires.
2. It is against God and it destroys one spiritually.
3. It causes separation from God here and forever.

C. Forgotten correction (vv. 31–32). Nebuchadnezzar refuses to correct his way of living. Refusing or ignoring warnings brings judgment. Note Galatians 6:7, 8. It was pride that destroyed Satan. See Isaiah 14:12–15.

II. The Punishment of Nebuchadnezzar (v. 33)

A. For seven years he lived with the animals. He ate with the oxen. His hair grew like eagle feathers. His nails grew like bird claws. The great king is now humbled! See also Proverbs 3:7; 26:12; Isaiah 5:21.

B. After seven years his sanity was restored. How foolish for us to think we can live without God. See Romans 1:21–32. God's judgment may be slow, but it will come.

III. The Pardon of Nebuchadnezzar (vv. 34–37)

A. Respect. God could have forgotten Nebuchadnezzar. However, God is filled with love and understanding.

B. Recognition (vv. 34–35). The first step toward God is to recognize our need. Verses 34 and 35 tell how he Nebuchadnezzar praised and worshiped and honored God.

C. Restoration (v. 36). Nebuchadnezzar's sanity returns and his kingdom is restored to him. Recognition of sin plus repentance brings restoration.

D. Respect (v. 37). "Now, I, Nebuchadnezzar, praise and glorify and honor the King of Heaven, the Judge of all, whose every act is right and good; for he is able to take those who walk proudly and push them into the dust!" (LB).

God was very patient with Nebuchadnezzar. He didn't have to give him the second chance. When man constantly rejects God, there is no guarantee that God will give him another opportunity to confess and forsake his sin. God could cut off such people suddenly (Prov. 29:1). Remember, God's patience is limited. It lasted just 120 years in Noah's time (Gen. 6:3). When God speaks, obey!

50

Belshazzar and the Finger that Spelled Death

Daniel 5:1–31

Babylon was a great city. It was fifteen miles square. It had enough food stored for twenty years. The wall around the city was 700 feet at the bottom and 300 feet at the top. Seven chariots side by side could race around the top of the wall. It was a great city, but it had forgotten God. Belshazzar did not learn from the mistakes of Nebuchadnezzar.

I. The Feast of Belshazzar (vv. 1–4)

A. Shame (v. 1). Belshazzar had a great feast. He invited many people to attend. He didn't invite God, but God attended anyway! Belshazzar drank his wine.

B. Sacrilegious (vv. 2–3). He used the vessels from the Temple to drink the wine.

C. Sin (v. 4). As they drank, the guests praised the idols of wood, gold, silver, brass, and stone. They knew this was wrong. See Exodus 20:1–7. See also Romans 1:21.

II. The Fear of Belshazzar (vv. 5–9)

A. Hand (v. 5). Suddenly a hand writes on the wall. The king sees this hand. God is speaking to him. Surely God spoke to him before, but he rebelled. See Proverbs 29:1.

B. Horror (v. 6). The fearless king is now filled with fear. All those present were filled with fear.

C. Helpless (vv. 7–8). All the wise men were called to interpret the dream. None knew the interpretation.

D. Hysterical (v. 9). All assembled saw the fearful king. He lost control of himself. He was confused and upset, not knowing the meaning of the dream. When we reject God, God sometimes uses drastic means to get our attention.

III. The Fate of Belshazzar (vv. 10–31)

A. The person (v. 12). Daniel is called to interpret the writing on the wall.

B. The punishment (vv. 17–25). Daniel reminds Belshazzar of how God humbled Nebuchadnezzar, causing him to eat grass like an animal. Daniel scolds Belshazzar for not remembering.

C. The prophecy (vv. 25–28). Daniel explains the words on the wall.

Mene—God has numbered thy kingdom and finished it.

Tekel—Thou art weighed in the balances and found wanting.

Peres—Thy kingdom is divided and given to the Medes and Persians.

D. The plight (vv. 29–31). As Daniel predicted, that very night Belshazzar's kingdom was taken from him.

Human history could be summed up in two words—"Forgetting God." Though there are many examples in the Bible, as well as daily examples of people forgetting God, we still do not seem to learn from them. If we don't bow willingly before God, we will have to bow by

51

Daniel and a Night with the Lions

Daniel 6:1–28

No one lives for God without being persecuted. No one lives for God without being misunderstood and criticized. Living for God requires dedication. Daniel had such dedication. A simple formula for a successful Christian life is: dedication, devotion, discipline, determination. Daniel had all of these qualities.

I. The Disposition of Daniel (vv. 1–5)

A. Preference (vv. 1–3). Daniel was chosen above others. He was different. Christians should be different (2 Cor. 5:17). Daniel had an excellent spirit.

B. Perfection (vv. 4–5). Not sinless perfection. Daniel pleased God in his living. See Matthew 5:48.

II. The Difficulty of Daniel (vv. 6–9)

A. The scheme. If anyone obeyed or served any other king he would be thrown to the lions. This was an effort to destroy Daniel. Persecution will come to all who live for God (2 Tim. 3:12).

B. The signing. The king, not fully understanding the motive behind the plan, signed his name. The order could not be changed. Stop praying or face the lions? What a choice!

III. The Decision of Daniel (v. 10)

A. Privacy—"He went into his house." Private praying (Matt. 6:6).

B. Pride—"His windows being opened." He was not ashamed.

C. Prayer—"He kneeled upon his knees three times a day." See James 5:16.

D. Praise—"He prayed and gave thanks." See 1 Thessalonians 5:18. Prayer is more than asking—it's thanking!
E. Practice—"As he did aforetime." Daily prayer (Ps. 55:17).

IV. The Danger of Daniel (vv. 11–17)

A. Plan disobeyed (vv. 11–15). Because Daniel prayed, he broke the king's law. The only time we may disobey man's law is when it keeps us from serving God.
B. Punishment for Daniel (vv. 16–17). Daniel is cast into the den of lions. He could have given up praying. But God was first in his life. See Matthew 6:33.

V. The Deliverance of Daniel (vv. 18–28)

A. Problem (vv. 18–19). The king could not sleep. He knew Daniel was a godly man, but he felt that he could not change his law.
B. Protection (vv. 20–22). The angel closes the mouth of the lions. God does protect his people. See Psalm 91.
C. Punishment (v. 24). Those who concocted the scheme to destroy Daniel are thrown in the den of lions and destroyed.
D. Prosperity (vv. 25–28). God made Daniel prosperous.

At times living for God may seem hard. But living for Satan is much harder. To live for God requires daily decisions, daily devotion, daily discipline, and daily determination. Daniel was not influenced by others. He made a personal choice to live for God. Don't allow family, friends, or pleasure to keep you from living for God.

New Testament Characters

52

Joseph—Jesus' Chosen Father

Matthew 1, 2

God needed a Christian husband and father for Mary and Jesus. God was really the Father of Jesus, but Joseph was the earthly father. Much emphasis is placed on Mary being the mother of Jesus, and how pure and holy she was. But what about Joseph? He, too, was a pure and holy person. He was a carpenter (Matt. 13:55). He kept the Jewish ordinances (Luke 2:21–24) and feasts (Luke 2:41). It appears that Joseph died before Jesus entered the ministry. Four times God spoke to Joseph.

I. Joseph and the Privacy for Jesus (Matt. 1:18–20)

A. Supernatural (v. 18). Mary and Joseph are now engaged, but Mary is expecting a child of the Holy Spirit. Isaiah (7:14) prophesied that a virgin would have a child. A supernatural birth!

B. Secret (v. 19). Joseph put Mary away. Note the words in Deuteronomy 22:25–28.

C. Spiritual (v. 20). An angel appears to Joseph, saying the child would be of the Holy Spirit to fulfill the prophecy in Genesis 3:15.

II. Joseph and the Plan for Jesus (Matt. 2:13–15)

A. Plan (v. 13). An angel appears telling Joseph to take Mary and Jesus into Egypt. God does lead. See Isaiah 30:21, and Proverbs 3:5, 6.

B. Place (v. 14). They family escaped to Egypt. They didn't question. God's ways are not our ways (Isa. 55:8).

C. Prophecy (v. 15). The family stayed in Egypt until Herod died, a fulfillment of Hosea 11:1.

III. Joseph and the Protection for Jesus (2:19–21)

A. Dream (vv. 19–20). An angel appears the third time to Joseph telling him to take Mary and Jesus back to Israel. Herod is now dead. Joseph was sensitive to the Holy Spirit, and because of this, he was led by God. We are told to walk in the Spirit (Gal. 5:16).

B. Dedication (v. 21). Joseph obeyed. Love for God is proved by our obedience (John 14:15). Note the words of Jesus in Luke 6:46.

IV. Joseph and the Prophecy of Jesus (2:22, 23)

A. Dream (v. 22). God appears in a dream to warn Joseph that Archelaus, son of Herod, and his wife Malthace were as brutal as Herod. Joseph is warned to take Mary and Joseph into Galilee rather than Judea.

B. Divine (v. 23). Joseph, Mary and Jesus settle in Nazareth. This would fulfill the prophecy. It is uncertain what is meant by "the prophets." Perhaps Nazareth is an unlikely place. See John 1:46, Isaiah 53, and Psalm 22.

A church, community, or nation can be no stronger than its men! The home needs strong husbands and fathers. The father and husband should be a strong Christian, a strong leader. He should be Christ-like. He should be spiritually-minded. Joseph set a good example as a father and husband. Unless the father is the head of the home, he is failing to obey God's plan for the home. A home where the father is not the head will be a failing home.

53

The Call of the Disciples

Matthew 10:1–17

The Bible tells how Jesus felt when he saw the many people without a Savior (Matt. 9:36). He asked that we pray for workers to finish his work. He needs volunteers in his work. He has always worked through human beings. In this passage we see Christ calling the twelve disciples. We can see the results of their work in Mark 16:16–20, as well as the Book of Acts.

I. The Calling of the Disciples (vv. 1–4)

A. The nature of the call (v. 1). Note the twofold power: (1) To overcome unclean spirits; (2) to overcome all sickness and disease (Mark 16:17, 18). Christians today have the same power from God. See Luke 24:49; Acts 1:8; 2:39.

B. The names of those called (vv. 2–4).

Simon Peter	Thomas
Andrew	Matthew
James	James
John	Thaddeus
Philip	Simon
Bartholomew	Judas

After Judas had betrayed Jesus and hanged himself, Matthias was chosen to take his place (Acts 1:26).

II. The Commission of the Disciples (vv. 5–16)

A. Purpose (vv. 5–6). Go to the lost sinners. See John 15–16.

B. Preaching (v. 7). Preach repentance (Acts 2:38) and the return of Christ (John 14:1–3).

C. Power (v. 8). Healing and evangelizing. Give yourself freely. See Isaiah 6:8 . . . "Send me."

D. Provision (vv. 9–10). Step out in faith. Expect God to meet your needs. Compare with Philippians 4:19, Psalm 37:25.
E. Peace (vv. 11–13). If the message is accepted, God will bless listeners, and the messenger. Don't waste time on constant rejections.
F. Punishment (vv. 14–15). Those who reject God and his Word will be rejected by God. Compare with Mark 16:16.
G. Persecution (v. 16). Sent as sheep among wolves. There would be danger. Be wise and sensible and harmless. Be sincere.

III. The Conflict Toward the Disciples (v. 17)

A. People would discourage them through criticism, gossip, lies, and so forth. They were challenged to be faithful (Rev. 2:10).
B. People would denounce them. See John 15:18, 19.
C. People would degrade them. Note Psalm 119:161, a prophecy about how Jesus would be persecuted without a real reason.
D. People would destroy them. Note the promise of Isaiah 59:19. Also see Isaiah 54:17.

God has called some Christians to be pastors or missionaries. He has called all Christians to be soul winners. Note Acts 1:8, ". . . and ye shall be witnesses unto me." We witness by the way we live, act, talk, and so forth. we also witness by word of mouth. Be more than a Christian—be a disciple. Obey all his teachings. See John 15:15.

54

A Selfish Request for James and John

Matthew 20:20–28

All people are born with selfish desires and feelings. When we become Christians these selfish desires are not destroyed. This is something we must do—overcome them daily. Paul speaks of the "inner man" (Eph. 3:16). This inner man will affect our actions and behavior. Paul says we must reckon ourselves (feelings and desires) as dead (Rom. 6:11). Note also we must crucify the "old man" (Rom. 6:6).

I. The Selfishness (vv. 20–22)

A. Seeking (v. 20). The mother of James and John came to Christ seeking a selfish desire. Note how to overcome selfishness (Gal. 2:20).

B. Sons (v. 21). The mother wanted her sons to sit at the right and left hand of Christ. She wasn't concerned with the sons of other mothers. She thought of herself only!

C. Supernatural (v. 22). "But Jesus told her, 'You don't know what you are asking!' Then he turned to James and John and asked them, 'Are you able to drink from the terrible cup I am about to drink from?' 'Yes.' they replied, 'We are able'" (LB).

II The Supernatural (v. 23)

A. Suffering. We are not able to suffer as Christ suffered, but we may suffer for him. See 2 Timothy 3:12. Suffering with Christ is a part of serving God (Luke 9:23).

B. Selection. "'Ye shall indeed drink from it,' he told them. 'But I have no right to say who will sit on the thrones next to mine. Those places are reserved for the persons my Father selects'" (LB).

III. The Shame (v. 24)

A. The disciples were angry because James and John were so proud. Note the words of Jesus in Matthew 18:4, that we must be humble and become like a child to enter heaven. James said we should humble ourselves (James 4:10).

B. The disciples were angry over the plan of James and John. The plan was selfish. Note Paul's words, "Not I, but Christ" (Gal. 2:20). No plans for others—just self!

C. The disciples were angry because of the selfish personality of James and John. Jesus said we should lose our life (Matt. 16:25). He should be first (Matt. 6:33). What we want is secondary.

IV. The Service (vv. 25–27)

A. Selfishness (v. 25). "But Jesus called them together and said, 'Among the heathen, kings are tyrants and each minor official lords it over those beneath him'" (LB).

B. Servant (v. 26). If you want to be great, then be a servant! Compare with Matthew 23:11.

C. Slavery (v. 27). "And if you want to be right at the top, you must serve like a slave" (LB).

The child of God should not seek selfish desires or advancement. Knowing God personally will mean that we seek to please him and do his will. Having the world's goods or possessions are all secondary when we seek to put him first in our lives and plans.

55

The Seven Sins of Peter

Matthew 26:33, 40, 51, 58, 69–72

Peter was great with words. However, his impulsive nature and living did not back up his words. Words are useless unless we practice them daily. Simply, "practice what you preach." Peter could boast about what he would do, but when the time came to stand for the Lord, he had no backbone and denied the Lord three times.

I. Self-sufficiency (v. 33)

A. Selfish pride. He did things in his own strength—not God's!

B. Selfish plan. He boasted as to what he would do.

C. Selfish person. Peter was unstable.

II. Sleeping (v. 40)

A. Unconcern. Peter was more concerned about physical comfort (sleep) than with helping Christ in his darkest hour.

B. Undedicated. Lack of dedication led to the denial of Christ.

C. Unprepared. He neither prayed enough nor prepared spiritually.

III. Self-esteem (v. 51)

A. Sin of anger. Christians shouldn't get angry. This is sin!

B. Sorrow of anger. Peter sought to kill Christ's enemies.

C. Spirituality or anger. Spiritual battles are won by spiritual means—not anger.

IV. Slothfulness (v. 58a)

A. He was fearful of what people would say, or think about him. This causes many people not to follow Christ closely.

B. Faithless. Peter was too weak to stand for Christ.
C. Fellowship. To have complete fellowship with Christ means a high price. Because of this, Peter didn't follow Christ closely.

V. Sensuality (v. 58b)
A. Easy way. Peter joined the crowd, following the easy way.
B. Exciting way. The world offers fun, but it's just for a short time.
C. Enticing way. Satan does not show the end—he shows the start and beauty of sin.

VI. Shame (vv. 69–70)
A. Peter denied Christ the Savior, man's only hope.
B. Peter denied Christ the sanctifier, the cleanser of all man's sins.
C. Peter denies Christ, who satisfies all man's needs.

VII. Swearing (vv. 71–72)
A. Sin always leads to sorrow. We can't sin without suffering. This sin will bring sorrow to others as well.
B. Pride leads to punishment. Pride always goes before a fall. Pride always separates from God.
C. Denial leads to destruction. If we deny Christ on earth, he will deny us.

After Peter's failure and denial, he was sorry and repented (Matt. 26:75). After Jesus arose from the dead, the angel at the tomb said, "But go your way, tell his disciples and Peter." (Mark 16:7). On the day of Pentecost, Peter preaches and 3,000 are converted. See Acts 2:14–17.

56

The Call of Matthew

Mark 2:13–20

God calls people to do his work. The ministry of Jesus lasted for only three years. During this time he called, taught, and trained the disciples and others to do his work. His work depends on the response to this call. In this passage we see God calling Matthew. God also explains what was involved in this call. Keep in mind that God could have called angels. Rather, he called man to do his work.

I. The Call by Christ (vv. 13–14)

A. The concern of Christ (v. 13). As the people followed Christ, he taught them. The last sermon of Jesus was a challenge to teach (Matt. 28:19, 20).

B. The call by Christ (v. 14). Matthew was a tax collector. They were known to be dishonest with the finances they collected. But when we follow Christ, he will make us what he wants us to be (Matt. 4:19).

II. The Concern by Christ (v. 15)

A. Evangelism. Note: "Many publicans and sinners sat also together with Jesus and his disciples." Jesus came to seek and save the lost. He didn't come to condemn—he came to convert and change. Not to judge but to justify.

B. Excitement. Note: "For there were many, and they followed him." Some followed because they were curious. Others followed because they were sincere. If one seeks God in sincerity he will find him (Jer. 29:13).

III. The Criticism of Christ (vv. 16–17)

A. Criticism (v. 16). Jesus was criticized for eating with sinners. To win sinners, one must love them. We love them as persons. We hate sin, but love the sinner! We must take the gospel to the sinner (Mark 16:15). Christ opposed the self-righteousness of the Pharisees (Matt. 5:20).

B. Conversion (v. 17). He came to save the lost. The Christian doesn't need Christ as Savior—the sinner does. The sinner is lost and must be born again (John 3:1–8).

IV. The Complaint to Christ (vv. 18–20)

A. The fasting (v. 18). Why didn't the disciples fast as John's disciples fasted? The Pharisees did much fasting, but much of it was for show—they were self-righteous. Note the boasting of the Pharisees in Luke 18:11–12.

B. The feasting (vv. 19–20). Do you fast at a wedding feast? After the death of Christ the disciples would fast.

As God called Matthew, so he calls others to do his work. Some are called to full-time ministry as ministers and missionaries. He calls others to serve as lay people, working within the church. The Christian cannot ignore the call of Mark 16:15 and John 15:16. Some Christians don't live close enough to hear his voice. Others hear but don't respond. Note Isaiah's response in Isaiah 6:8. Compare with v. 14, how Matthew arose and followed. No demands or promises—he followed!

57

The Rich Young Ruler

Mark 10:17–22

A young man comes to Jesus seeking the way to heaven. Humans have always sought a way to God. There is only one way to heaven (John 14:1–6). There is a way that seems right to man, but the end is death (Prov. 14:12). God has made the way to heaven so simple that all may understand (Isa. 35:8). If they are sincere, seekers will find the way to God (Jer. 29:13).

I. The Request by the Young Ruler (v. 17)

A. Respect—"And kneeled to him." He showed respect to Christ as the Son of God. It is important that we fear and respect God. Compare with Ecclesiastes 12:13.

B. Request—"Good master, what shall I do that I may inherit eternal life?" The jailer at Philippi made a similar question (Acts 16:30). Note how Nicodemus came seeking Christ in John 3:1–8.

II. The Response to the Young Ruler (v. 18)

A. Goodness—"And Jesus said unto him, why callest me good?" Christ shows his humility. He points to God—not himself!

B. Godly—"There is none good but one, that is, God." Paul says God's goodness should lead to repentance (Rom. 2:4).

III. The Rules Given to the Young Ruler (vv. 19–21)

A. Commandments (v. 19). Six commandments are listed. Jesus said all the Ten Commandments could be summed up in the words of Matthew 22:37, 39. Apparently the rich man didn't keep the first and second commandment.

B. Completion (v. 20). He kept six of the Ten Commandments from his youth. Had he kept the first and second commands, he would have known Christ. We cannot love God with all our hearts without pleasing God and keeping all the commandments.

C. Command (v. 21).
   1. Savior—"Then Jesus beholding him loved him." Note the love of Christ in John 3:16, Romans 5:8.
   2. Sincere—"One thing thou lackest." He needed Christ. Keeping some of the commands are not enough! See Romans 3:23.
   3. Sharing—"Go thy way, sell whatsoever thou hast and give to the poor." Put Christ first (Matt. 6:33). See also 1 John 3:17.
   4. Sacrifice—"Take up the cross, and follow me." Compare with Galatians 2:20 and Luke 9:23.

IV. The Rejection of the Young Ruler (v. 22)

A. Riches—"And he was sad at that saying." He loved his possessions more than God. Note the difficulty of a rich man entering into heaven (Matt. 19:24).

B. Regret—"And went away grieved: for he had great possessions." Note the words of Jesus in Mark 8:36. There is no indication that the rich man ever accepted Christ.

There are three pictures of a rich man in the Bible. Could this be the same man? (1) He comes as a young man to Christ. (2) The rich farmer with his barns full (Luke 12:16). (3) The rich man being in hell (Luke 16:19). There is no proof this is the same man, but it could be. Riches are not wrong—they are wrong only when they separate us from God.

58

Zacharias and Elisabeth

Luke 1:1–19

Zacharias was a priest. He was a spiritual man. He was humble and poor. He and his wife had no children. Both were growing old. A childless couple was considered a shame. Zacharias was faithful to God all his life. God blesses those who are faithful. Note the promise of faithfulness in Revelation 2:10. Faithfulness has a twofold influence: (1) a concern for God; (2) a consecration to God.

I. The People of God (vv. 1–7)

A. Proof (vv. 1–). The key verse here is v. 4. Note the word *know* which is so important. We must know the truth. Compare with John 8:32, John 14:6. Also we must study to know (2 Tim. 2:15).

B. People (v. 5). The priest Zacharias and his wife Elisabeth.

C. Purity (v. 6). Note the lives of Zacharias and Elisabeth.

1. They were righteous. Compare with 1 Timothy 6:11.
2. They walked in all the commandments. See John 14:15.
3. They were blameless. See Philippians 1:10.

D. Childless (v. 7). This presented a problem. Both were old. It meant also a reproach among the people at that time.

II. The Plan of God (vv. 8–12)

A. Work (vv. 8–9). Zacharias was busy at work, burning incense in the Temple. This was done twice a day—in the morning and at 3:00 p.m. (Exod. 30:7, 8).

B. Worship (v. 10). All the people were praying at this time. They were looking forward to the fulfillment of Genesis 3:16.

C. Wonder (vv. 11–12). The angel appears unto Zacharias.

Zacharias is fearful. He falls on his face before the Lord in respect toward God.

III. The Promise by God (vv. 13–17)

A. Promise (v. 13). Zacharias and Elisabeth would have a son. His name would be John, meaning, "The Lord is gracious or shows grace."

B. Prophecy (vv. 14–17)

1. Rejoicing (v. 14). Many would rejoice at his birth (John 1:29–36).
2. Righteous (v. 15). He would be great. He wouldn't drink any strong drink. He would be a Nazarite (Judg. 13–15).
3. Repentance (v. 16). Many would repent and turn to God through John the Baptist. See Luke 3:1–9.
4. Revival (v. 17). John would prepare the way for the coming of Christ. See Luke 3:16–17.

IV. The Power of God (vv. 18–19)

A. Problem (v. 18). Zacharias was old. It was impossible now to have a son. He remembers how God gave Abraham a son in old age. See Hebrews 11:6; Genesis 21:1–5.

B. Power (v. 19). Gabriel the angel said he was sent by God to Zacharias to tell this good news.

John the Baptist was blessed by having godly parents. The lives of the parents have an effect on the children. Note the words of Proverbs 22:6, "Train up a child in the way he should go: and when he is old, he will not depart from it." John was used of God to introduce Christ. Had Zacharias and Elisabeth been poor examples perhaps John would have grown up and not been used by God.

59

John Prepares the Way for Christ

Luke 1:11–19; 3:2–6, 19–20

John the Baptist was the Elijah of the New Testament. He was born about six months before Jesus. John would prepare the way for the coming of Christ. Note these words, "Behold the Lamb of God, which taketh away the sins of the world" (John 1:29). John would baptize Jesus in water (John 1:33). Note more about John in Mark 1:1–6.

I. The Personality of John (1:11–19)

A. Prophecy. "'Listen: I will send my messenger before me to prepare the way. And then the one you are looking for will come suddenly to his Temple—the Messenger of God's promises, to bring you great joy. Yes, he is surely coming,' says the Lord of hosts" (Mal. 3:1, LB).

B. Promise. It was given to Zacharias, the father of John whose name means "Remembered by the Lord." John's birth is a foreshadow of the birth of Christ. See Luke 1:76, 77.

C. Personality (Luke 1:11–19).

1. Prayer (vv. 11–14). Prayer is heard. The name of the child would be John. Many would rejoice at his birth.
2. Personality (vv. 15–16). He would be great in the sight of the Lord and filled with the Spirit from birth. Note the result of the Spirit-filled life (Gal. 5:22, 23).
3. Preparation (v. 17). He would be like Elijah, the Elijah of Malachi 4:5, 6.
4. Possibility (vv. 18–19). Zacharias was old and was made speechless for doubting that he would have a son. He remained speechless until eight days after John was born (Luke 1:57–64).

II. The Preaching of John (3:2–6)

A. Preaching (v. 3)

1. Repentance. Compare with Jesus' words of Luke 13:3.
2. Baptism. Note Luke 3:3, and Acts 2:38.
3. Judgment. Note the words of Luke 3:7, 9.
4. Christ's coming. See Luke 3:16 and Acts 19:4.
5. Son of God. See John 1:34, the eternal existent Christ.
6. Salvation. Jesus the Lamb of God, taking away the sin of the world (John 1:29).
7. Holy Spirit. He (Jesus) would baptize with the Holy Ghost. See Mark 1:8, Acts 1:5.

B. Picture (vv. 4–6). "In the words of Isaiah the prophet, John was "a voice shouting from the barren wilderness, 'prepare a road for the Lord to travel on! Widen the pathway before him! Straighten the curves! Smooth out the ruts! And then all mankind shall see the Saviour sent from God'" (LB). See Isaiah 40:3, 4.

III. The Persecution of John (3:19, 20)

A. Sin (v. 19). Herod had taken his brother's wife, Herodias. He broke commandment seven (Exod. 20:14). See Leviticus 18:16.

B. Suffering (v. 20). John was placed in prison for one year. Jesus sends encouraging words to John (Luke 7:22–35).

C. Slaughter (Matt. 14:1–12). Herodias' daughter asks for the head of John after she danced before the king.

John was used of God to lead many to salvation. Note how John did not do miracles (John 10:41). He did not have a long ministry. He met with death because he was faithful to God. He risked his life by exposing the sin of Herod. He was faithful until death. See Revelation 2:10.

60

Mary—the Mother of Jesus

Luke 1:46; 2:1–7

Mary was the mother of Jesus. She was not perfect and without sin. Though she was the mother of Jesus, she showed the proper respect to him as the Son of God. The worship of Mary is unscriptural. Mary, as all people, was a sinner (Rom. 3:23). Mary accepted the assignment to be the mother of Jesus. She was not forced into it.

I. The Divine Praise (1:46–50)

A. Praise (vv. 46–47). Praise is important and necessary. Mary praises God. Compare with Psalm 100 and 150:6.

B. Person (v. 48). God chose Mary, a humble person, to be the mother of Jesus. Mary will fulfill the Scriptures of Genesis 3:15, "The seed of the woman." She will fulfill the teaching of a virgin having a child. (Isa. 7:14)

C. Pleasure (v. 49). God would do great things through Mary. The Son of God, the Messiah, would come through her. Mary accepted the will of God as Jesus did (Matt. 26:39).

D. Promise (v. 50) His mercy is eternal. Note Psalm 100:5, how his mercy is everlasting.

II. The Divine Plan (1:51–56)

A. Power (vv. 51–52). "'How powerful is his mighty arm! How he scatters the proud and haughty ones! He has torn princes from their thrones and exalted the lowly'" (LB).

B. Provision (v. 53). He meets man's needs. Note the Old Testament promise in Psalm 37:25. Then look at the promise of the New Testament (Phil. 4:19).

C. Promise (vv. 54–55). All God's promises are true. See Numbers 23:19. He keeps his promise and sends the Messiah. See Galatians 3:14–16.

D. Protection (v. 56). "Mary stayed with Elizabeth about three months and then went back to her own home" (LB).

III. The Divine Person (2:1–7)

A. Perfection. Some churches teach that Mary was perfect. The Bible does not teach this. Mary did not ascend into heaven as some teach. This teaching takes away worship to Jesus Christ.

B. Plan (vv. 1–4). Joseph and Mary go to Bethlehem to pay tax or for the census. Note v. 5, Mary and Joseph are engaged. They would have no physical relationship until after Jesus was born. She would fulfill Isaiah 7:14.

C. Pregnancy (vv. 5–6). While in Bethlehem, God chose this as the time and place for Jesus to be born. The Son of God born in a barn! What humility.

D. Poverty (v. 7). Note "first born." Mary bore at least four brothers and two sisters (Matt. 13:55, 56). After the birth of Jesus, Mary and Joseph were married.

Mary bore Christ. She trained him. He was baptized at the age of thirty. He taught for just three years. Mary was at the crucifixion and the resurrection. She was one of the 120 to enter the Upper Room to pray for the promise of Luke 24:49. Mary was an excellent model of a wife and mother. She is an example in obedience and holiness, a great woman used of God because she was fully surrendered to God.

61

Simeon and Anna

Luke 2:21–38

Jesus, the Son of God, becomes the Son of Man. Through this he could have feelings toward mankind. John tells how the Word became flesh (John 1:14). In this passage we see Jesus being brought to the temple to be dedicated. Jesus was not baptized until he was thirty. Then he began his ministry. Note the two important godly people in this passage—Simeon and Anna.

I. The Divine Presentation (vv. 21–27)

A. Purification (vv. 21–23). The Jewish law didn't permit a woman to leave her home for forty days after she gave birth. See Exodus 13:2; Numbers 18:5.

B. Presentation (v. 24). The poor could offer turtle doves or pigeons in the place of a lamb (Lev. 5:11). The extreme poor could offer a couple quarts of flour.

C. Person (v. 25). Simeon was a just and devout person. He was waiting for the Messiah. The rabbis called the Messiah consoler or comforter.

D. Promise (v. 26). The Holy Spirit revealed to Simeon he would not die until he saw the Messiah. See Amos 7:7.

E. Parents (v. 27). Mary and Joseph bring Jesus to the temple for dedication. Dedication of children is a safe and scriptural practice for both parents and children.

II. The Divine Prophecy (vv. 28–35)

A. Pleasure (vv. 28–30). Simeon is now pleased he has seen the Messiah—the salvation of the Lord. This is a fulfillment of Isaiah 12:2; Psalm 27:1.

B. Preparation (vv. 31–32). Simeon saw the Lord personally.

We may know him personally. See Philippians 3:10; Psalm 23:1.

C. Prophecy (v. 33). What Simeon said was given by the Holy Spirit. The Holy Spirit does reveal to God's people certain things. See John 16:13.

D. Power (v. 34). Through Christ many would find salvation and forgiveness of sin. See Romans 10:13; 1 John 1:9.

E. Problems (v. 35). Many who appeared to be Christians would be insincere. This would pierce the heart of Jesus.

III. The Divine Praise (vv. 36–38)

A. Person (v. 36). Anna a prophetess. She was elderly. She had lived with her husband for seven years. God used women in the Old Testament as prophetesses.

B. Personality (v. 37). She was now a widow. She was eighty-four years old and remained in the temple. She served God with fastings and prayers. Note: she was daily in the temple. She enjoyed the house of God. Compare with Psalm 122:1; Hebrews 10:25.

C. Praise (v. 38). She gave thanks and praise to God. She speaks of the Messiah, who is Jesus in the form of a baby.

Just as Anna and Simeon gave thanks and praise because they had seen the Messiah, so should we offer praise and thanksgiving for the many times we see Jesus the Savior revealed to us as we read Scripture, meditate on it, or listen to the preaching of the Word.

62

The Appearance of John the Baptist

Luke 3:1–18

John the Baptist appears as was promised. He is the Elijah of the New Testament. He comes to prepare the way for Christ, the Messiah. He is an evangelist, preaching repentance. He warns the listeners to repent of his sin and turn to God. Note John 1:6, "There was a man *sent from God* whose name was John."

I. The Personality of John (vv. 1–6)

A. Person (vv. 1–2). John the son of Zacharias.

B. Preaching (v. 3). John preaches the baptism of repentance for sin. Compare Luke 13:3.

C. Prophecy (vv. 4–6)

1. Preparation (v. 4). Prepare the way of the Lord. Get ready to meet him. Note the words of Amos 4:12.
2. Prophecy (v. 5). "Level the mountains! Fill up the valleys! Straighten the curves! Smooth out the ruts" (Isa. 40:3–5, LB).

II. The Preaching of John (vv. 7–11)

A. Preparation (v. 7). Warning to flee the judgment of God. Perhaps referring to Revelation 20:11–15. See also John 5:24.

B. Personal (v. 8). Straighten up your lives. Get right with God. Compare with John 3:3, 2 Corinthians 5:17, Hebrews 12:14.

C. Punishment (v. 9). If we do not produce fruit, then we will be destroyed. Compare with John 15:5–7.

D. Plan (vv. 10–11). Share what you have with others. See 1 John 3:17. Put your love into action.

III. The People and John (vv. 12–18)

A. People (vv. 12–13). Publicans ask how they may be ready to meet God. Answer: Be honest and don't collect more taxes than you turn in.

B. Peace (v. 14). Be content with your pay. Compare with Philippians 4:11; Hebrews 13:5.

C. Person (v. 15). The people were looking for the Messiah. They wonder if John is the Messiah. Was he the one Genesis 3:15 spoke of?

D. Prophecy (vv. 16–17)

1. Power (v. 16). Jesus would baptize with Holy Spirit. See John 1:33.
2. Purging (v. 17). The wheat (Christians) go to heaven. The chaff (sinners) go to hell. Compare with Mark 16:16.

E. Preaching (v. 18). John preached and exhorted the people.

John was a fearless preacher. He was willing to fully obey God. He was placed in prison for his forthrightness and later beheaded. God worked through John because he was fully surrendered unto God. He was willing to fully obey God, though it meant suffering and even death.

63

The Good Samaritan

Luke 10:25–42

Christians should be willing to help others. Often Christians are so busy with selfish plans that they neglect to help others. The Christian life is more than getting—it's giving! In John 6 we see people following Christ because he gave free food. We also see these people leaving him (John 6:66). There is a price to pay (Luke 9:23).

I. The Sincere Seeker (vv. 25–28)

A. The desire (v. 25). A man comes to Christ, seeking the way to heaven. Note the simple way to heaven (John 3:1–8).

B. The demand (vv. 26–27).

1. Love God with all our hearts—our feelings.
2. Love God with all our souls—our spiritual being.
3. Love God with all our strength—our physical love.
4. Love God with all our minds—our thought life.

Then love our neighbors as we love ourselves. Compare with 1 John 3:17. Loving God makes it easy to love others.

C. The destiny (v. 28). Keeping this command means we are keeping the Ten Commandments (Exod. 20:1–17).

II. The Simple Symbol (vv. 29–35)

A. The problem (vv. 29–30). A traveler was robbed, wounded, and left to die. He was hurt deeply, he needed help.

B. The people (vv. 31–35). Note the people who came by:

1. Priest. He represents the religious world. Offering no help, he had a form, but no reality. See 2 Timothy 3:5.
2. Levite. He represents the church world. He was too busy to help. No doubt a social engagement kept him busy. The church should meet spiritual needs first—not social needs!

3. Samaritan. This represents the Christian world. Those who know God will help. See 1 John 3:17.

C. The pity. Here we see the pity shown by the Samaritan. Others ignored the wounded man. The Samaritan stopped to help. He had God's love within him.
   1. Divine love. He had compassion on him.
   2. Practical love. He bound up his wounds.
   3. Kind love. He took the victim to an inn to be taken care of and helped.
   4. Unselfish love. He paid for the victim's care and medication.

III. The Simplicity Shown (vv. 36–42)

A. Application (v. 36). Who is your neighbor? The one who needs help. All who need our help physically or spiritually are our neighbors.

B. Answer (v. 37). Note Jesus' words, "Go and do thou likewise." Don't talk about love—show it! Jesus said if even our enemy is hungry we must feed him (Prov. 25:21). See also Matthew 5:42 and Luke 12:33.

C. Affection (vv. 38–42). Showing our love and worship toward the Lord is needed. Sometimes we can be so busy serving that we have no time to pray or worship the Lord.

Are you a good Samaritan? Do you help those in need? Are you willing to use your time and money to help others? Follow these simple steps:

1. Be considerate. Think of others. Think of their needs and problems.
2. Be consecrated. Give yourself to Christ, and let him work through you.
3. Be compassionate. Put yourself in the place of others.
4. Be Christ-like. Christ loved and helped all. We should do the same.

64

The Rich Farmer

Luke 12:13–34

Some people judge success by earthly possessions. God judges success by heavenly possessions. God keeps a record of all we do as Christians and will reward us (Mal. 3:16). The more faithful we are, the greater our reward will be. Jesus speaks in verse 34 of sending up a treasure to heaven. If our minds are on heavenly things we will be busy doing things for God. See Colossians 3:1, 2.

I. The False Riches (vv. 13–15)

A. Riches (vv. 13–14). Man has always been interested in money. Money is not evil, but the love of money is evil (1 Tim. 6:10).

B. Reality (v. 15). Genuine riches means not the amount of your wealth, but enjoying the riches you have. Not being satisfied leads to coveting. Coveting is disobeying the Tenth Commandment (Exod. 20:17). Coveting is a deceptive, destructive, and damning sin.

II. The Foolish Reasoning (vv. 16–19)

A. The man's success (vv. 16–17). He had very good crops. He was successful in planning and preparing the good crops.

B. The man's selfishness (vv. 18–19). "And finally exclaimed, 'I know—I'll tear down my barns and build bigger ones!' Then I'll have room enough. And I'll sit back and say to myself, 'Friend, you have enough stored away for years to come. Now take it easy! Wine, women, and song for you.'" (LB) Note the personal pronouns, *I* and *my* appear eleven times in this story.

III. The Final Results (vv. 20–21)

A. Death (v. 20). Note that God calls this man a fool. Remember, we cannot take our possessions with us when we die (1 Tim. 6:7).

B. Deception (v. 21). "Yes, every man is a fool who gets rich on earth but not in heaven" (LB). If we have Christ, we are rich. We have a heavenly home. Note these words, "Some rich people are poor, and some poor people have great wealth" (Prov. 13:7, LB).

IV. The Faithful Reliance (vv. 22–26)

A. Worry (vv. 22–23). Don't worry about what you will eat, wear, or where you will live. God will take care of these concerns for you. See Philippians 4:19.

B. Wonder (v. 24). Stop to consider the wonderful way that God cares for the birds. We are more important than the birds. Compare with Psalm 37:25.

C. Worthless (vv. 25–26). Does worry help? Of course not! Learn to cast all your care on him. See 1 Peter 5:7.

V. The Father's Resources (vv. 27–34)

A. Flowers (v. 27). God gives beauty to the flowers. All of Solomon's riches couldn't match their beauty.

B. Faith (vv. 28–30). We must trust in God, put him first in our lives. He will meet our needs. Note the importance of faith (Heb. 11:6).

What are we doing for God with our possessions? Are we sharing in our giving? Are we paying our tithes? (Mal. 3:8–10) There is the danger for the Christian to love money and commit sin (1 Tim. 6:10). God wants our money and he wants our life! Note the words of Paul in Romans 12:1, 2. He wants all our love (Matt. 22:37). When we put him first in our lives, then we are truly rich.

65

The Rich Man and Lazarus

Luke 16:19–31

There are just two places after death—heaven or hell. God gives all a choice as to where they will go after this life. Some people say this is just a parable. In parables Jesus never gave people's names as he did in this story. Look at these scriptures about hell. (1) Wicked sent to hell (Ps. 9:17). (2) Everlasting punishment (Dan. 12:2). (3) The people in hell (Rev. 21:8). (4) No rest in hell (Rev. 14:11; 20:10).

I. The People in this Story (vv. 19–21)

A. Man of wealth (v. 19). "There was a certain rich man," Jesus said, "who was splendidly clothed and lived each day in mirth and luxury" (LB). [*Dives* is the Latin word for rich].

B. Man of want (vv. 20–21). "One day Lazarus, a diseased beggar, was laid at his door. As he lay there longing for scraps from the rich man's table, the dogs would come and lick his open sores" (LB).

II. The Pain and the Separation (vv. 22–26)

A. Heaven (v. 22). "Finally the beggar died and was carried by the angels to be with Abraham in the place of the righteous dead. The rich man also died and was buried" (LB).

B. Hell (v. 23). "And his soul went to hell. There, in torment, he saw Lazarus in the far distance with Abraham" (LB).

C. Help (v. 24). The rich man cries out for water to cool his tongue because of the torment in hell. See Matthew 25:46.

D. Helpless (v. 25). Too late to change now. He had the opportunity on earth, but rejected it. See Hebrews 9:27. Also note Revelation 20:11–15.

E. Horror (v. 26). Once in hell there is no chance to escape. No second chance! It will be everlasting punishment (Rev. 20:10).

III. The Plea from the Sufferer (vv. 27–31)

A. The pain (vv. 27–28). "Then the rich man said, 'O Father Abraham, then please send him to my father's home—for I have five brothers—to warn them about this place of torment lest they come here when they die'" (LB). See Revelation 14:11. On earth this man had no time for God, now he wants to send a missionary to earth to warn his brothers.

B. The prophets (v. 29). "But Abraham said, 'The scriptures have warned them again and again. Your brothers can read them any time they want to'" (LB). There is no excuse for man to be lost.

C. The proposal (v. 30). The rich man thought if someone rose from the dead, his brothers would believe him. Later, Christ rose from the dead and people didn't believe him.

D. The problem (v. 31). If the brothers did not believe Moses and the prophets, they would not believe if someone rose from the dead. His people rejected Christ (John 1:11). Note the words of Isaiah 53:3.

Besides hell, there is heaven. Notice some verses from the Bible about heaven.

1. The words of Jesus (John 14:1–6).
2. A home not made with human hands (2 Cor. 5:1).
3. Abraham looked for a city made by God (Heb. 11:10).
4. Paul spoke of being with Christ after death (2 Cor. 5:8).
5. The Bible tells of a new heaven (Rev. 22:1–7). God gives you the choice. Which will it be?

66

Zacchaeus's Salvation and Restitution

Luke 19:1–10

Christ came to save all people. It is his will that all be saved (2 Peter 3:9). Note the word *whosoever* in John 3:16 and Romans 10:13. After Zacchaeus accepted Christ, he made restitution. Repentance makes us right with God—restitution of what we took by force or fraud, plus damages, makes us right with those whom we have victimized.

I. The Personality of Zacchaeus (vv. 1–4)

A. The passing (v. 1). Jesus passes through Jericho. He enters this town to preach. He loved all people. See Matthew 9:36.

B. The personality (v. 2). Zacchaeus was the chief among the publicans. The publicans were tax collectors. Most were dishonest with the money they collected.

C. The person (v. 3). Zacchaeus was a short man. As Jesus passed through town, he wanted to see him. Note the desire of Paul toward Christ (Phil. 3:10).

D. The persistence (v. 4). He ran and climbed a sycamore tree. Note Job's desire to know God (Job 23:3).

II. The Pity Toward Zacchaeus (vv. 5–6)

A. The command (v. 5). Christ was interested in Zacchaeus. Note: "I must abide at thy house." Does Christ live at your house? Compare with Josh. 24:15.

B. The conversation (v. 6). Zacchaeus came down from the tree and was received joyfully by Christ. Those who accept Christ are made sons of God (1 John 3:2; John 1:12).

III. The Prejudice Toward Zacchaeus (v. 7)

A. Self-righteousness. The people complained because Jesus ate at a house of a sinner. Jesus came to save sinners. He didn't come to condemn—he came to convert. See Matthew 18:11.

B. Sinners received. The woman in adultery was forgiven by Christ (John 8:11). Note his words, "Neither do I condemn thee: go, and sin no more."

C. Salvation received. Note the words of Jesus in John 6:37. He accepts all who repent. He forgives all sin (1 John 1:7).

IV. The Pardon of Zacchaeus (vv. 8–10)

A. Restitution (v. 8). He would give one-half of his possessions to the poor. If he took money wrongly, he would repay fourfold.

B. Reception (v. 9). Salvation came to Zacchaeus. Though he was a sinner, all his sins were forgiven (Ps. 103:3).

C. Redemption (v. 10). Here we see the mission of Jesus. He loved the world and gave himself (John 3:16). Look at his great love (John 15:13). See also Jeremiah 31:3.

Salvation is the start of life "in Christ." After we are right with him we make things right with others. We cannot be right with God and not right with fellow human beings. Our prayers will be hindered if we fail to make restitution. Remember four of the Ten Commandments are toward God; six are toward our neighbors whom we must love as we love ourselves.

67

Andrew—the Soul Winner

John 1:35–42; 6:1–14

Everyone knows how God used Peter. Though Peter had denied Christ three times (Matt. 26:69–75), he was sorry and repented. God used one of Peter's sermons to convert 3,000 people (Acts 2:37–41). Few of us remember that it was Andrew who won Peter to Christ. In the eyes of God, both Peter and Andrew are equal. Through history many unknown people have been used of God to win someone who was used by God to win thousands to Christ.

I. The Curiosity of Andrew (1:35–39)

A. Statement (vv. 35–36). John the Baptist is speaking, telling of the power of this blood (1 Peter 1:19). We are forgiven of all sins through this blood (1 John 1:7).

B. Sincerity (v. 37). The two disciples (Andrew and John, the son of Zebedee), hear, and follow. Those who accept Christ become sons of God (John 1:12).

C. Seeking (vv. 38–39).

1. Question (v. 38). "Jesus looked around and saw them following. "What do you want?' he asked them. 'Sir,' they replied, 'where do you live?'" (LB)

2. Answer (v. 39). "'Come and see,' he said. So they went with him to the place where he was staying and were with him from about four o'clock that afternoon until the evening" (LB).

II. The Conviction of Andrew (1:40–42)

A. Person (v. 40). Andrew, Peter's brother. He meets Christ personally. David speaks of God being a personal God.

B. Personal (v.41). Andrew after meeting Christ shares good news with his brother, Peter. Note these words, "Go home to thy friends, and tell them how great things the Lord hath done for thee" (Mark 5:19). Andrew witnessed at home, fulfilling Mark 16:15.

C. Promise (v. 42). "And he brought Peter to meet Jesus. Jesus looked intently at Peter for a moment and then said, 'You are Simon, John's son—but you shall be called Peter, the rock'" (LB).

III. The Consecration of Andrew (6:1–14)

A. Problem (vv. 1–7). Many people followed Christ to hear him preach and teach and perform miracles. They were hungry with nothing to eat.

B. Provision (vv. 8–9). Andrew had some faith. He had located a boy with five loaves and two fish. Faith is necessary (Heb. 11:6).

C. Plan (vv. 10–11). The people are told to sit in small groups. All their needs would be met. See Philippians 4:19.

D. Plenty (vv. 12–13). After feeding five thousand (Matt. 14:20–21), the leftovers were gathered in twelve baskets. Compare with Psalm 37:25.

E. Prophet (v. 14). The people recognize Christ as a prophet. See also John 7:40.

God does not call all Christians to be ministers or missionaries, but he does call all to be soul-winners! Had Andrew not won Peter perhaps many would never know Christ. One need not have talent to be a soul-winner. Andrew allowed God to use him to win Peter to Christ—Peter in turn won thousands to Christ!

68

Lazarus Comes to Life

John 11:1–44

Christ came to give life. He never conducted a funeral service. Note his words, "I am come that they might have life" (John 10:10). He wants to give us abundant and enjoyable life. Those who follow him are never sorry. We do not really enjoy life until we accept Christ as Savior. He not only gives us abundant life, he also gives us eternal life (John 3:16; 5:24).

I. The Problem Before Christ (vv. 1–4)

A. People (vv. 1–2). Lazarus was sick. His sisters Martha and Mary were close friends of Jesus. This was not the same Lazarus mentioned in Luke 16:19–31. Note how Mary serves or ministers unto Christ. Christ seeks this from all his people.

B. Plea (v. 3). They ask Christ to come and heal Lazarus.

C. Purpose (v. 4). Christ says this sickness is for the glory of God. Compare with Romans 8:28.

II. The Procrastination by Christ (vv. 5–16)

A. Postponing (vv. 5–6). Though Christ knew Lazarus was sick, he did not leave immediately. God's delays are not denials.

B. Plan (vv. 7–8). Jesus plans to return unto Bethany. He knew it meant persecution from the Jews.

C. Protection (vv. 9–10). As long as Christ walked in the light of God's will, he was safe. Compare with 1 John 1:7.

D. Prediction (vv. 11–14). Christ says Lazarus was asleep and that he would awaken. We too shall awaken (1 Thess. 4:13–18).

E. Power (vv. 15–16). Because Christ wasn't there to heal Lazarus, now he can demonstrate his power and raise him from the dead.

III. The Promise by Christ (vv. 17–26)

A. Problem (vv. 17–19). Lazarus was buried two days ago.

B. Plea (vv. 20–21). Martha tells Jesus if he had been there, Lazarus would not have died. She didn't have faith. See Hebrews 11:6.

C. Promise (vv. 22–24). Jesus promises to bring Lazarus back to life again. Only he had this power.

D. Power (vv. 25–26). The giver of life also has the gift of life. Compare with John 5:24. Martha does believe that he is the promised Messiah.

IV. The Personality of Christ (vv. 28–37)

A. Response (vv. 28–29). Martha secretly calls Mary and she comes quickly.

B. Respect (vv. 30–32). Mary bows and worships him.

C. Reasoning (vv. 33–37). Christ shows compassion and concern. Jesus weeps.

V. The Power of Christ (vv. 38–44).

A. Command (vv. 38–39). "Remove the stone from the tomb."

B. Christ (v. 40). If one believes, he or she will see God's power (Matt. 19:26).

C. Confirmation (vv. 41–42). The confirmation that God heard him was made for the sake of the people standing around the tomb.

D. Complete (vv. 43–44). Lazarus, who was bound, comes forth.

Do you have life in Christ? Do you have abundant and enjoyable life? Do you have the joy that comes with this life? The psalmist foretells the joy in Christ (Ps. 16:11). Allow Christ to control your life, then you will not only have enjoyable life but also the promise and hope of eternal life in heaven.

69

Mary's Sacrificial Love

John 12:1–9

Mary sets a proper example for all to follow. She gave her self, savings, and service. She gave her best—her time. God wants our money, but first he wants our time. He wants our service. Though the perfume was expensive, Mary felt that nothing was too good to give to Christ. She gave because she loved him.

I. **The Situation (vv. 1–2)**
   A. Place (v. 1). Jesus comes to Bethany. It was six days before the passover.
   B. People (v. 2). A meal is prepared for Jesus. Mary and Martha were there. Lazarus was there also. Jesus had earlier raised him from the dead (John 11:39–44). These three were close personal friends of Jesus.

II. **The Sacrifice (v. 3)**
   A. "A jar of costly perfume." Some experts estimate that a person would have to work 300 days to make enough money to buy that perfume.
   B. "And anointed Jesus' feet with it and wiped them with her hair." We too should worship Christ with our gifts.
   C. "And the house was filled with fragrance." Our life should leave a pleasant impact. Note Acts 11:26.

III. **The Selfishness (vv. 4–6)**
   A. Complaint (vv. 4–5). "Should not the perfume have been sold and the money given to the poor?" Not necessarily. When Christ is first in our lives, we will joyfully worship him with our gifts. That doesn't mean that we neglect giving for the poor. See Matthew 6:33.

B. Character (v. 6). Note Judas' character. "Not that he cared for the poor, but he was in charge of the disciples' funds and often dipped into them for his own use!" (LB)

IV. The Savior (vv. 7–8)

A. Rebuke (v. 7). *The Living Bible* says, "Let her alone, she did it in preparation for my burial." Don't be critical of those who live sacrificial lives in serving God.

B. Respect (v. 8). "You can always help the poor, but I won't be with you very long" (LB). Christ would soon leave (John 16:7–11). While he is here, serve him.

V. The Supernatural (v. 9)

A. Some of those present responded with curiosity only; others were sincere. Christ honors the seeking heart (Jer. 29:13). Compare with Proverbs 3:5, 6.

B. Supernatural (v. 9b). "And also to see Lazarus." The people wanted to see the supernatural. Christians should not follow and seek the supernatural—the supernatural should follow our lives.

God wants what's first—not what's left. Christians should honor the Lord with the firstfruits of their finances (Prov. 3:9). Mary didn't only talk about her love—she also showed it. If we love him, we will obey him and his commands (John 14:15). One of his commands is that he be first in our life (Matt. 6:33). Give to Christ your best—your life and time.

70

Doubting Thomas Believes

John 20:24–31

"Doubting Thomas" refused to believe Christ arose from the dead until he saw and felt his hands. Doubt and unbelief destroy faith in Christ. The closer we are to Christ, the greater faith we will have. We must have faith in God, faith in ourselves, and faith in others.

I. The Absence of Thomas (v. 24)

A. Absence shows a lack of desire. Thomas apparently had no desire to be with the other disciples. There should be a desire to attend God's house (Ps. 122:1)

B. Absence shows a lack of dedication. Thomas lacked dedication. When we are dedicated, we want to attend God's house. Compare with Hebrews 10:25.

C. Absence shows a lack of discipline. Thomas did not practice discipline to overcome his doubts.

II. The Attitude of Thomas (v. 25)

A. Faithless—"Except I see." Hebrews 11 tells of the great heroes of faith who believed before they saw.

B. Faith (Heb. 11). Faith believes before it sees. Note Hebrews 11:6. We don't have to understand—just trust.

C. Fellowship. Fellowship with other Christians will encourage our faith. Thomas' absence discouraged his faith.

III. The Effect of Thomas (vv. 26–28)

A. Appearance of Christ (v. 26). Jesus appears to the disciples even though the doors and windows were locked. He has a heavenly body. We too will have such a body (1 John 3:2).

- B. Appearance of Christ (v. 27). "Then he said to Thomas, 'Put your finger into my hands. Put your hand into my side. Don't be faithless any longer. Believe'" (LB).
- C. Response to Christ (v. 28). "My Lord and my God." The same personal relationship as David had in Psalm 23:1.

IV. The Acceptance of Trust (v. 29)

- A. Faith when you see (v. 29a). This is really not faith. Note "O thou of little faith" (Matt. 14:31).
- B. Faith when you don't see (v. 20b). This is true faith. Note Hebrews 11:1, "The evidence of things *not seen*."

V. The Attitude of Trust (vv. 30–31)

- A. Result of faith (v. 30). "Jesus' disciples saw him do many other miracles besides the ones told about in this book." Compare with John 21:25.
- B. Reason for faith (v. 31). "But these are recorded so that you will believe that he is the Messiah, the Son of God, and that believing in him you will have life."

How does one obtain faith? Paul says "faith cometh by hearing, and hearing by the Word of God" (Rom. 10:17). This faith will help you overcome the world (1 John 5:4). Note also the words of Paul, "Whatsoever is not of faith is sin" (Rom. 14:23). Faith in God will cause doubt to flee. However, too much doubt causes faith to flee.

71

Peter's Restoration

John 21:15–23

Peter denied Christ three times. After his denial, he was sorry and wept. When one fails God, God is concerned. He is forgiving. If one sins and is sorry, God forgives (1 John 1:9). Note the words of 1 John 2:1, 2. If we sin we have an advocate or an attorney to plead our cause. Of course, we should not sin willfully. When we become Christians, we should resist sin and temptation and live an overcoming life.

I. The Affection (vv. 15–17)

A. Jesus asked Peter three times if he loved him. Peter replied that he did. Jesus then asked him to feed his sheep. True love for God is based on our obedience to him. Note the words of Jesus in John 14:15. If we love him—obey him. If we love him—share him.

B. Character (v. 17). Jesus knew all about Peter, he knew his real character. In v. 17 from *The Living Bible,* "Lord you know my heart." Peter boasts he would never offend Christ (Matt. 26:33). Note Jesus' words, "That this night before the cock crows, thou shalt deny me thrice" (Matt. 26:34, LB). Note the three denials of Peter (Matt. 26:69–75), and how Peter weeps and is sorry.

II. The Acceptance (vv. 18–19)

A. Desire (v. 18). "When you were young, you were able to do as you liked and go wherever you wanted to; but when you are old, you will stretch out your hands and others will direct you and take you where you don't want to go" (LB).

B. Direction (v. 19). Note the words of Jesus, "Follow me." No promises—just simply, "Follow Christ." Then look at the denials of Peter (Matt. 26:39–75). Because Peter didn't follow closely, he denied Christ. Note that he slept when he should have been praying (Matt. 26:40). He followed afar (Luke 22:54).

III. The Attitude (vv. 20–23)

A. Attitude (v. 20). Peter was concerned about the other disciples. Who was the disciple who would betray Jesus? Was this a form of self-righteousness? Note the words of warning against self-righteousness (Luke 18:11–12).

B. Attention (vv. 21–23). Jesus was saying in simple words, "Don't worry about the other disciples. Take care of yourself." Note these words, "If I want him to live until I return, what is that to you? You follow me" (v. 22, LB). Some people are so busy judging others that they don't take care of their own lives.

After Jesus arose the angel said, "But go your way, tell his disciples and Peter" (Mark 16:7). The angel wanted Peter to know that Christ forgave him for his denial. Peter was sorry—he repented. Judas was sorry—sorry that he was caught. He didn't repent. If we are truly sorry for our failures and shortcomings, Christ will forgive. However, we must be sorry enough to stop sinning and change our lifestyle.

72

Matthias, the Thirteenth Disciple

Acts 1:12–26

God has always used humans to do his work. He chose Moses, Joshua, the judges, kings, prophets, the disciples, and even people today to do his work. Judas was a disciple, but he was a counterfeit Christian and betrayed Christ (Luke 22:47–54). In this passage we see a selection of a disciple to fill Judas's place.

I. Prayer (vv. 12–14)

A. After the ascension, the disciples returned to Jerusalem to the upper room to fulfill Luke 24:49. The men and women continued in prayer. The 120 disciples would pray for ten days before Acts 2:14 came to pass.

II. Peter (v. 15)

A. The response of Peter (Matt. 14:18–22). Peter obeys the call.
B. The rejoicing of Peter (Matt. 17:4). Peter was with James and John on the Mount of Transfiguration with Christ.
C. The rejection by Peter (Matt. 26:69–75). He denies Christ.
D. The resurrection and Peter (Mark 16:7). Note how Christ tells the people to go and tell Peter he arose and forgave Peter.
E. The repentance of Peter (Matt. 26:75). Peter truly repents.

III. Prophecy (vv. 16–20)

A. Verse 16 refers to Psalm 41:9. Judas was with Christ for three years. He preached, cast out devils, healed the sick. Now he turns against Jesus.
B. Compare with Psalm 69:25–28. Judas lost three things: his salvation, his Savior, and his soul.

IV. Problem (vv. 21–22)

A. Christ chooses twelve disciples to carry on his work (Mark 3:14–19). All had different personalities. All would learn God's work and carry on after the ascension of Christ.

B. Judas betrays Christ. Someone is needed to fill his place. Man may fail God, but God's work goes forward.

V. Plan (vv. 23–26)

A. People (v. 23). "The assembly nominated two men: Joseph Justus (also called Barsabbas) and Matthias" (LB).

B. Prayer (vv. 24–25). "Then they all prayed for the right man to be chosen, 'O Lord,' they said, 'you know every heart; show us which of these men you have chosen as an apostle to replace Judas the traitor, who has gone on to his proper place" (LB).

C. Person (v. 26). Matthias is selected. The disciples are now known as The Twelve. God knows who is qualified to do his work. It is he who does the calling and preparing.

Note verse 24 carefully, how the people prayed for wisdom and direction. Too often in the selection of persons to do God's work, we look at personality. We look at popularity. Do we really seek God's will? Note how David sought God's will (Ps. 143:10). God hears us when we pray, if we pray according to his will (1 John 5:14).

73

Suffering of the Apostles

Acts 5:17–42

The apostles suffered much for doing God's will. They were willing to preach the gospel, even though that endangered their lives. They had an excitement that could not be silenced. The prisons could not stop them. The beatings could not stop them. The fire of God burned in their hearts as with Jeremiah (Jer. 20:9).

I. The Degradation of the Apostles (vv. 17–23)

A. Degradation (vv. 17–18). They are placed in prison, Jesus foretold that this would happen (Matt. 24:9–10).

B. Deliverance (vv. 19–20). God delivers them. God does deliver (1 Sam. 17:37; Dan. 6:22). God told them to continue preaching even though this was the reason for their imprisonment.

C. Departure (vv. 21–23). The officers didn't know they were out of prison. The prison doors were shut and guarded. Compare with Psalm 91:3.

II. The Declaration by the Apostles (vv. 24–27)

A. The apostles after deliverance from prison continue to preach the gospel. Persecution couldn't stop them.

B. "The police captain went with his officers and arrested them (without violence, for they were afraid the people would kill them if they roughed up the disciples) and brought them in before the Council" (LB).

III. The Determination of the Apostles (vv. 28–32)

A. The command (v. 28). "'Didn't we tell you never again to preach about this Jesus?' the High Priest demanded. 'And instead you have filled all Jerusalem with your teaching and intend to bring the blame for this man's death on us'" (LB).

B. The comment (v. 29). "We would rather obey God more than man." Compare with John 14:15. The apostles were told to go to the temple and preach (v. 20). They obey!

C. The Christ (vv. 30–32). Christ is the reason for the continued preaching. God sends up Christ. The Jews crucify him. God exalts him. He arises from the dead (John 20:1–31). He ascends into heaven (Acts 1:9–11). The people were witnesses of this.

IV. The Denunciation of the Apostles (vv. 33–42)

A. Plan (v. 33). The rulers plan to kill them. The authorities couldn't stop the excitement, so they seek to kill the apostles. Compare with Matthew 24:9.

B. Protection (vv. 34–39). Note the wisdom in Gamaliel's words: if what they teach is not of God, it will die. If of God, we are fighting God!

C. Persistence (vv. 40–41)
   1. The authorities agree with Gamaliel. The apostles are beaten and let go. Note 2 Timothy 3:12.
   2. The apostles rejoiced and praised God. They were willing to suffer with him. See Romans 8:17.
   3. They could not stop preaching the gospel. Compare with 1 Corinthians 9:16.

The church enjoys so much freedom today as the result of the suffering of the apostles. God's work goes forward when he finds people who are willing to stand and to work for him. Doing God's work could mean suffering physically. It could mean persecution from family, relatives, and friends. If it does, stand for God. He will stand with you.

74

Stephen—the Spirit-filled Layman

Acts 6:1–15

Every layperson should give time and talent to God. In some areas, pastors do the work laypeople should be doing. God constantly seeks people to do his work (Ezek. 22:30). In this passage we see how God worked through Stephen, a dedicated layman.

I. Problems in the Church (v. 1)

A. The condition (v. 1a). The Church grew and multiplied. Compare with Acts 2:41–47. When God's commands are followed, we will have God's results.

B. The complaint (v. 1b). ". . . there were rumblings of discontentment. Those who spoke only Greek complained that their widows were being discriminated against, that they were not being given food, in the daily distribution, as the widows who spoke Hebrew" (LB).

II. Plan of the Church (vv. 2–8)

A. Problem (v. 2). The apostles were busy serving tables. They didn't have time to search God's Word and to pray. God calls his servants to a "spiritual ministry"—not to do laypeople's work.

B. Plan (v. 3). The church wanted seven men with these characteristics:

1. Honest report (Prov. 22:1)
2. Full of the Holy Spirit (Eph. 5:18; Acts 2:1–4).
3. Full of wisdom (James 1:5; 1 Cor. 12:8).

C. Prayer (v. 4). The apostles wanted to continue to give

themselves wholly to prayer (Acts 2:1–4; James 5:16). and to the ministry of God's Word (Mark 16:15; 2 Tim. 4:2–4).

D. People (vv. 5–7). The apostles laid hands on the seven chosen men and prayed. God's Word grew and multiplied.

E. Practice (v. 8). Note the character and work of Stephen. He was full of the power of faith (Zech. 4:6). Great wonders and miracles were performed (physical and spiritual).

III. Persecution of the Church (vv. 9–15)

A. Sinful people (vv. 9–10). Certain stubborn members of the synagogue refuse to accept Stephen's words. They debate with him. Note verse 10, how they could not resist the wisdom of the Spirit in his speaking. God's Word is powerful (Heb. 4:12).

B. Sinful plan (vv. 11–14). They lie, saying Stephen was blasphemous against Moses and God. They stir up the people, the elders and scribes.

C. Surrendered person (v. 15). The members of the council who condemned Stephen saw his face shine. Compare with Psalm 34:5; Daniel 12:3. When we spend time with Christ, there will be a difference in our appearance and lifestyle.

God's work needs surrendered laypeople such as Stephen. The church today needs people like Stephen to carry forth God's work. People should (1) have an honest report, an honest character and an honest life; (2) be full of the Holy Spirit, and evidence the fruits of the Spirit (Gal. 5:22, 23); (3) be full of wisdom. With such people in our churches, our churches will be filled with God's power and his Spirit.

75

Stephen's Sermon and Death

Acts 7:1–60

Stephen was one of the seven deacons chosen in Acts 6:5. He was not an apostle—he was a layman. God worked through him, performing many miracles (Acts 6:8). His love and dedication to God led to his death. In this passage we hear Stephen's sermon, which was from God's Word, and its rejection, leading to his death.

I. The Sermon by Stephen (vv. 1–50)

A. He spoke of the past of God's people, Israel.
B. He spoke of the protection of God's people, Israel.
C. He spoke of the provision of God's people, Israel.
D. He spoke of the plan of God's people, Israel
E. He spoke in the power of the Holy Spirit.

II. The Application in Stephen's Sermon (vv. 51–53)

A. He called the rulers "stubborn" (v. 51). These people resisted God's Spirit as their forefathers did.
   1. They resist the prophecy of Christ (Isa. 53:3).
   2. They resist the pardon of Christ (John 1:11).
   3. They resist the preaching of Christ (Luke 4:28, 29).
B. He called the rulers "murderers" (v. 52). Their forefathers persecuted and killed the prophets. These prophets told of the coming Messiah. Compare with Hebrews 11:37. They rejected God back in the time of Moses (Heb. 11:24–26). The rulers continued the rejection of the "Just one."
C. He called the rulers "rejectors." "Yes, and you deliberately destroyed God's laws, though you received them from the hands of angels" (LB). They had the Ten Commandments (Exod. 20:1–17). They didn't keep them. They tried to

force the Jewish ceremonial laws on the people. Jesus didn't come to destroy the law, but to fulfill it (Matt. 5:17).

III. The Surrender of Stephen (vv. 54–60)

A. Problem (v. 54). "The Jewish leaders were stung to fury by Stephen's accusation, and ground their teeth in rage" (LB). The Holy Spirit's conviction brings anger.

B. Personal (vv. 55–60). Stephen was full of the Holy Ghost. He sees Jesus standing at the right hand of God. Normally he is seated (Heb. 1:3). Jesus stands ready to welcome Stephen home to heaven.

1. Stephen is run out of town and stoned.
2. Reception—"Receive my spirit." Now Stephen would have everlasting life with Christ (John 3:16).
3. Remission—"Lay this sin not to their charge." Note the importance of forgiveness (Eph. 4:32, Matt. 5:44).

God's people do suffer persecution (Matt. 5:10–12). Godless people will not understand the Christian's love and dedication to God. Because of this, there will be persecution and perhaps even death.

76

Saul Becomes Paul

Acts 9:1–22

Saul watched as Stephen was stoned to death. He held the coats of those who did the stoning (Acts 7:58). Paul persecuted the Christians (Acts 8:3). In this passage we see Saul meeting Christ and we discover how Saul's life is changed. He is changed from Saul the persecutor to Paul the preacher. Paul will become one of the all-time great preachers.

I. Pardon for Saul (vv. 1–6)

A. Suffering (vv. 1–2). "But Paul, threatening with every breath and eager to destroy every Christian, went to the High Priest in Jerusalem. He requested a letter addressed to synagogues in Damascus, requiring their cooperation in the persecution of any believers he found there, both men and women, so that he could bring them in chains to Jerusalem" (LB).

B. Surprise (vv. 3–4). He meets the Lord. God brings people down willingly or unwillingly. See Philippians 2:10, 11.

C. Savior (vv. 5–6). "'Who is speaking, sir?' Paul asked. And the voice replied, 'I am Jesus, the one you are persecuting! Now get up and go into the city and await my further instructions'" (LB).

D. Surrender (v. 6). Note Paul's surrender. "Lord, what wilt thou have me to do?" Later, Paul preached this surrender (Rom. 12:1, 2.) He was told to go and wait for the Lord.

II. Prayer for Saul (vv. 7–16)

A. Speechless (vv. 7–9). "The men with Paul stood speechless with surprise, for they heard the sound of someone's voice but saw no one! As Paul picked himself up off the ground, he found that he was blind. He had to be led into Damascus and was there for three days, blind, going without food and water all the time" (LB).

B. Special Person (vv. 10–12). There was a disciple of Christ named Ananias. God told him to pray for Paul's healing.

C. Stalling (vv. 13–14). Ananias is fearful to do this, since he remembers Paul as a persecutor of Christians.

D. Servant (vv. 15–16). Saul was God's chosen vessel to bring the gospel to the Gentiles. Note Paul's words (Rom. 1:16). Later, he would suffer for the sake of Christ (2 Cor. 11:24–28).

III. Preaching by Saul (vv. 17–22)

A. Prayer (v. 17). Ananias lays hands on Paul and Paul is healed. Note God's plan for healing (Mark 16:18; James 5:13–15).

B. Perfection (vv. 18–19). He was healed because of obedience. Obey Mark 16:18 and you will get Mark 16:20 results.

C. Preaching (v. 20). Paul immediately preached the gospel. He obeyed the command of Mark 16:15.

D. Power (vv. 21–22). The people were amazed at Saul's preaching. Just a short time ago he was persecuting Christians (Acts 9:1–2). Now he is saved and preaching the gospel.

God had to make Paul blind to get his attention. Then he used Ananias to pray for his healing. Note how Paul immediately preached the gospel after meeting Christ. His life was completely changed (2 Cor. 5:17). Now that he is saved, he spreads the newness of life with others. God uses Paul because he fully surrenders himself to God (Acts 9:6).

77

Mark—a Devoted Disciple

Acts 12:12–25; 13:13; 15:37–39

Most experts feel that Mark was a very young man when he wrote the Gospel of Mark. It is the shortest of the four gospels. Little is known of Mark. He seems unstable and immature at times. The young man fleeing (Mark 14:51–52) is perhaps Mark. Though Mark may not have been stable, he dedicated his life to God, and was used of God.

I. The Family of Mark (12:6–17

A. Peter in fetters (vv. 6–7). Peter is in prison for preaching the gospel. James was with Peter, and was beheaded (12:1, 2).
B. Peter is freed (vv. 8–10). An angel leads Peter out of prison. There is freedom in Christ for all God's people. See John 8:32, 36.
C. Power of fellowship (vv. 11–12). The church was united in praying for Peter at Mark's home. There is great power in united prayer (Matt. 18:19).
D. Problem of fear (vv. 13–17). The people didn't believe Peter was free. Faith is important to please God (Heb. 11:6).

II. The Fear of Mark (12:18–23)

A. Deliverance (vv. 18–19). The people were amazed at Peter's deliverance. There were sixteen guards protecting him. These guards were put to death.
B. Deception (v. 20). Herod speaks and the people say he is a god (v. 22). Jesus spoke of deception in Matthew 24:4–5, 11, 24. Mark faced all this in his day.
C. Destruction (v. 23). God strikes Herod dead, because he didn't give glory to God. See the evils of boasting described (James 4:16; Prov. 25:14).

III. The Fulfillment of Mark (12:24–25)

A. Word of God (v. 24). God's Word grew. See Isaiah 55:10–11. See also Hebrews 4:12; Joshua 1:8.

B. Work of God (v. 25). Barnabas and Paul take John Mark with them. They fulfill Mark 16:15. Mark would gain experience from being with these Christian workers.

IV. The Failure of Mark (13:13)

A. Mark's work. Mark served with Barnabas and Paul for an unknown time. They heard the call of Matthew 4:19.

B. Mark's wrong. Why did Mark quit? His reasons could have been persecution, disappointment, or misunderstanding. Other people left Jesus (John 6:66).

V. The Forgiveness of Mark (15:37–39)

A. Disagreement (vv. 38–38). Paul didn't want Mark with him. Perhaps he was immature. To work together, two must agree. See Amos 3:3 and Psalm 133:1.

B. Decision (v. 39). Barnabas takes Mark with him. He proved to be a success. Note: "Take Mark, and bring him with thee: for he is profitable to me for the ministry" (2 Tim. 4:11).

Later Peter was a great help to Mark. No doubt Peter remembered his own failures and denials of Christ, and later Christ's forgiveness. Mark had some problems, but he seemed to overcome them and wrote the Gospel of Mark. God can take failures and rejection and make them succeed in his work. Peter and Mark are two examples.

78

Paul and Silas

Acts 16:16–40

All Christians find it easy to rejoice when they are in good health. It's easy to be satisfied when you have employment and everything is going your way. However, during trouble, problems, and disappointments, the real Christian emerges. Not only were Paul and Silas in prison—they were also beaten and placed in stocks. Despite all these difficulties, they could sing praise to God at midnight.

I. The Rejection (vv. 16–24)

A. Sinful person (vv. 16–17). A fortune teller, who was a demon-possessed slave girl, earned much money for her master.

B. Spiritual power (v. 18). Paul cast out her demons.

C. Sinful plan (vv. 19–21). The master of the fortune teller now lies about Paul and Silas. Christ said we would be hated for the sake of the gospel (Matt. 24:9). Even though you may be hated, keep in mind that God is on your side (Isa. 54:7).

D. Suffering persecution (vv. 22–24). Paul and Silas were whipped and placed in prison, and in stocks. Note the sufferings of Paul in 2 Corinthians 11:24. God's people will suffer. See John 15:18, 19.

II. The Rejoicing (vv. 25–34)

A. Praise (v. 25). Though in pain, at midnight Paul and Silas could sing praise to God. Paul speaks of the importance of singing in Ephesians 5:19. See also James 5:13; 1 Corinthians 14:15.

B. Problem (vv. 26–28). There was an earthquake. The prison doors are open. The jailer was upset, ready to kill himself.

C. Pardon (vv. 29–32). Note the question in verse 30—"What must I do to be saved?" Then the answer in verse 31—"Believe in the Lord Jesus Christ." See Romans 10:9, 10, 13.

D. Peace (vv. 33–34). The whole family of the jailer was converted and baptized. Compare with Acts 2:38, and the words of Jesus in Matthew 28:19, plus the words of Paul in Romans 6:14.

III. The Release (vv. 35–40).

A. Regret (vv. 35–36). The judge sent the police to free Paul and Silas. They recognized that these men were falsely accused. Note how when we please God even our enemies are at peace with us (Prov. 16:7).

B. Requirement (v. 37). "But Paul replied, 'Oh, no they don't! They have publicly beaten us without trial and jailed us—and we are Roman citizens! So now they want us to leave secretly? Never! Let them come themselves and release us'" (LB).

C. Report (vv. 38–39). The authorities were afraid because Paul and Silas were Roman citizens. They begged them to leave the city.

D. Reaction (v. 40). Though they were put in prison for preaching the gospel, Paul and Silas continued to preach. Compare with Jeremiah 20:9. They go to Lydia's home.

Paul and Silas revealed true Christianity. This attitude brought conviction and conversion. They could have complained. They could have felt sorry for themselves for their pain and suffering. Instead, they showed a deep relationship with God. The Spirit of God within them was greater than the suffering from without. Therefore, they could rejoice in service to God. As a result, an entire family was brought to Christ.

79

Aquila and Priscilla

Acts 18:1–4, 18–26

Many people had a vital part in the ministry of Paul. Aquila and Priscilla were two such helpers. There are many dedicated people who work behind the scenes. People like this make God's work a success. They may not be recognized by man, but they are by God. As Aaron and Hur held up Moses' hands (Exod. 17:11–13), so we need people to hold up the hands of God's workers. God sees such work and will reward the faithful for such service.

I. Working and God (vv. 1–4)

A. Place (v. 1). Paul came from Athens to Corinth. Paul was led and directed by God. Compare with Psalm 37:23.

B. People (v. 2). Aquila was a Jew and Priscilla was Roman. They fell in love and were married. Her name is mentioned six times in the Bible. Claudius was emperor of Rome.

C. Practical (v. 3). Paul lived with Aquila and Priscilla and worked with them as tentmakers. Paul supported himself financially. Compare with 2 Thessalonians 3:10.

D. Preaching (v. 4). Every Sabbath Paul was in the synagogue seeking to win the Jews and Greeks to Christ. Paul was obeying Mark 16:15. Aquila and Priscilla were impressed by him.

II. Working for God (vv. 18–23)

A. Parting (vv. 18–19). Paul, Aquila, and Priscilla stay in Corinth for eighteen months. As Paul taught, Aquila and Priscilla remained in Ephesus.

B. Pleading (vv. 20–22). The Jews in the synagogue pleaded with Paul to remain longer, but he had to move on. Paul was an evangelist—not a pastor. Note Paul's words in 2 Timothy 4:5.

C. Preaching (v. 23). Paul leaves Jerusalem and goes to Galatia and Phrygia to strengthen the disciples.
Aquila and Priscilla were not ministers—just ordinary Christian workers. Paul refers to them in 1 Corinthians 16:19; Romans 16:3, 4.

III. Working with God (vv. 24–26)

A. Person (vv. 24–25). Apollos. He was an eloquent man (great speaker), mighty man in the Scriptures. He knew God's Word. He practiced 2 Timothy 2:15. He was fervent in spirit. He had great enthusiasm, as did Jeremiah (Jer. 20:9). He taught the things of the Lord diligently. He was a student of God's Word (1 Peter 3:15).

B. Preaching (v. 26). Apollos speaks boldly in the synagogue. Aquila and Priscilla help teach him "The way of God perfectly." One must know his Word to teach it clearly (2 Tim. 2:15).

God wants his workers to be "fervent in spirit." See Romans 12:11. The word *fervent* actually means "to boil." God wants his people to be on fire for him. He began the church with fire (Acts 2:4). Aquila and Priscilla worked together as a dedicated couple, fulfilling the command of God. Allow God to use you as this couple did working behind the scenes for the glory of God.

80

Paul—God's Servant

Galatians 1:1–24

Paul was one of the great preachers! See him before his conversion (Acts 8:1–4). Something happened to Paul. He meets Christ (Acts 9:1–6). His life is changed. Now a converted zealous persecutor is fervently preaching the gospel. He is whipped, stoned, placed in prison, yet he could not give up Christ (Acts 20:24). He could sing while in prison (Acts 16:25). He writes many epistles while in prison, encouraging Christians to live a godly life.

I. The Call of Paul (vv. 1–5)

A. Person (v. 1). Note: "Paul the Apostle"—not of men, neither by man, but by Jesus Christ. Compare with John 1:6, how John was sent by God. God called and sent Paul to minister.

B. People (vv. 2–3). Greetings to all people. Grace and peace from the Father.

C. Power (v. 4). By giving himself for our sins, he freed us from this evil world. Compare with Isaiah 53:5, 6; 2 Corinthians 5:17.

D. Praise (v. 5). Glory and praise to God. Practice Psalm 100.

II. The Concern of Paul (vv. 6–9)

A. Problem (v. 6). It is easy to go back to old habits and practices and behaviors. See John 6:66. Note "Another Gospel"—something other than truth.

B. Perversion (v. 7). "For there is no other way than the one we showed you; you are being fooled by those who twist and change the truth concerning Christ" (LB).

C. Pitfall (vv. 8–9). If anyone preaches something other than the gospel, God's curse should be on him. He repeats in v. 9 what he says in v. 8.

III. The Consecration of Paul (v. 10)

A. The Danger of Pleasing Men (v. 10a). Note the danger of pleasing men (John 12:43). Felix pleased the people and persecuted Paul (Acts 24:27).

B. The Delight of Pleasing the Master (v. 10b). Christ must be first in our life (Matt. 6:33). We cannot serve two masters (Matt. 6:24).

IV. The Communication of Paul (vv. 11–17)

A. Authentic (vv. 11–12). Paul's message came from Jesus Christ. We are told to preach the gospel (Mark 16:15). Not our words, but God's Word.

B. Ancestral (vv. 13–14). Paul described his past, how he followed the old Jewish laws and regulations.

C. Amazing (vv. 15–17). Before Paul was born, God's hand was upon him. God needed him to preach the gospel. When Paul was called to preach, he did not seek man's opinions—he went and preached!

V. The Conduct of Paul (vv. 18–24)

A. Preaching (vv. 18–19). Paul did not seek out the disciples, except James. He was called, so he preached. When God calls—obey! He will help us, and give us strength (Phil. 4:13).

B. Praise (vv. 20–24). People remember how Paul had persecuted the Christians . . . now he is praising God and preaching the gospel. Note verse 24, how the people glorify God through Paul.

Paul's great success began when he met Christ. He asked, "Lord, what wilt thou have me to do?" He teaches us to give our life to God (Rom. 12:1–2). As we yield to God, he will work through us. He may not use us in the same way as he used Paul, but he will use us for his glory.